Harrison Carter

Investing While Young

The How-To-Book of When to Invest
for Massive Long-Term Gains

CRUCIAL TREATS
USA

Copyright 2020 by CRUCIAL LLC – All Rights Reserved

In no way is it legal to reproduce, duplicate, or transmit any part of this document in either electronic means or in printed format. Recording of this publication is strictly prohibited and any storage of this document is not allowed unless with written permission from the publisher. All rights reserved.

Respective authors own all copyrights not held by the publisher. The information herein is offered for informational purposes solely, and is universal as so. The presentation of the information is without contract or any type of guarantee assurance.

The trademarks that are used are without any consent, and the publication of the trademark is without permission or backing by the trademark owner. All trademarks and brands within this book are for clarifying purposes only and are owned by the owners themselves, not affiliated with this document.

Contents

Introduction	1
Financial Freedom	8
Investing	21
Self-Evaluation	34
Timeline	47
Location	62
Winners vs. Losers	73
History	83
Game Time	98
Residual Income	110

I
Introduction

Today, millions of smart investors are waking up without the dull ring of an alarm clock dreading the hours they have to spend doing work they dislike. Even more so, people are living their lives with passion, vigor, and enthusiasm. And the main reason is that they chose a new and sometimes challenging path towards living a lifestyle they wear with a hint of pride. Yet, this book is not about sharing the dream life with you; of course, that will be the outcome of what I will discuss. This book is about making investments of time, money, and knowledge work for you. If you want simple, this is not the book for you. Nor, is it a get rich quick scheme. But, if you wish to see incremental results for a positive financial future, then you may be facing a road to real success.

Let me ask you this. Where do you see yourself in 15-20 years? Where are you living? Are you working and do you own a house? Have you traveled and seen the world? Are you living life how YOU want to live?

If you've answered these questions honestly, you will find that these pertinent questions spring up a dream life for you. They make you see how you want your life to come to look in the future. That is a great thing, and it's certainly possible if you are willing to take the time to work for this life. Let's consider your parents, who worked for 20-30 years during a challenging financial climate. Yet if they made the smart investment, you might be the recipient of those investments. Naturally, your parents knew that the best investment is adequate planning and action from their end. Alternatively, if you weren't that fortunate to have been born into a life of luxury, it's perfect that you have decided to make your way and start your life off on the right note.

I've committed my life and time to learn all about investing, and I've seen great investments, and I've seen poor ones. That said, I've also made significant investments that have helped move me professionally and personally to new heights. Yet, I've taken some pretty big falls too. Many people ask me the question: "What does it take to retire early?" There are so many ways to answer this very question, and you will be exploring the answers in this book with me.

Our journey together will be a fruitful one, as we take a walk through the vines of investing fundamentals. I want to answer your question: "What is investing?" with a straight forward and engaging explanation in chapter 1. This critical question will bring you to a pleasant realization that investing is a process that can be learned. So, if you're willing to take the needed time and genuinely get into the details, you will undoubtedly find the doors of investment open up to you.

The reality is that when you know the meaning of investing and what it entails, you will be surprised to find that your perspective shifts in new and exciting pathways. Along with perspective shifts, you will feel confident with the knowledge and also amazed at the possibilities. You may want to share this newfound knowledge with everyone you know, and that's always a good thing to do. Yet, before you start sharing, you should have proof that it works, and you only really get this by applying the fundamentals you will learn within these pages.

Learning and applying your knowledge will be a crucial factor that will determine your success as an investor. You have to make that shift in mindset to be ready to sail the waves of change.

I will share insights into a variety of topics, and an essential issue will entail a discussion about investment in you in chapter 2. This is a discussion that you hardly ever get the chance to be involved in, perhaps you were too young at the time, or financial freedom was not something you were considering. Since you've picked up this book, I know that the timing will be perfect for you as you learn the trade secrets housed within these chapters of personal knowledge that I'm finally going to share with you.

During my mentor sessions, I'm always interested in finding out how excited my new students are about learning investment strategies. The reality is they want to jump right in and genuinely start seeing the rewards. So, I want to remind you that along with financial freedom for life comes patience and making a substantial investment in your growth and development as an investor. You must nurture your investing knowledge and prioritize your learning in this area. You will be pleased to find that investing in yourself is the key to unlocking vast levels of investing knowledge that's available out there. And I'll show you practically how to do this.

In the third chapter, I'll discuss the importance of timing your investment well. You may have heard the saying that timing is everything, and it becomes even more apparent as I write this amidst the global pandemic that has alarmed every sector of the economy. It's fascinating to see how the economic fabric has changed with a single event, and I'll add that this is not the first time we have seen the market fluctuate due to sudden catastrophic events. I'll show you exactly how you can turn these events that bring anxiety and fear into everyone around you into an opportunity in the investment space.

These next few chapters alone should be compulsory reading for every college graduate. In these sections, you will see the exact steps I used to invest proactively. You will get an inside look into where to invest.

I have to add that I've often found that enthusiastic investors lose their spark when trying to find the exact places to invest. I certainly do not want that for you. To help, I've included the best places to start investing and give you the right foundations with a small investment. The exciting news is that technology has created accessible frameworks for investors to take advantage of and use effectively. Now that you've whet your appetite in the investment field, it's time to dig in and get into the details in chapters 5, 6, and 7.

You get introduced to a winning strategy as you enter chapter 5, and I can tell you that it has worked like a charm for many other investors. It's a tool that, when applied well, and consistently can help you quickly build up your investment portfolio, and see large increments over 10 to 15 years. This is what the greatest investors of our time have used to build their wealth from humble beginning to 6, 7 or 8 figure incomes. I'll also share some detailed trends into well-known companies and how they have trended over a 10 to 20 years period. It will open your eyes to new ways of viewing these companies, especially from an investor's eye.

Of course, if you enjoy the details and data shared in the winning strategy for investment success, you will be blown away by how companies you know win the market.

You will undoubtedly find it interesting how you can attach yourself to these opportunities early in the game and hold on patiently to see the multiplication of your initial investment. History is a great storyteller, and I believe it can give you unique insights into the future of investing. Therefore, chapter 6 will bring light to companies like Apple, Microsoft, and more. As you follow along, you may, at this point, be wondering: "When will I get to the actual investing bit?"

That is undoubtedly part of your investment journey, but before you do that, I have a few strategies to share on the companies to look at and what you should be looking for exactly. You can expect details around the characteristics of a good company, and what to look for with their financials and of course where to find these financials. I'll give you the critical insights that investors know about companies that thrive long term, and you will know by the end of chapter 7, how to go about picking winning companies for your investments.

You can expect eye-opening advice on winning investments, investing trends, and how to ensure you always succeed at investing. You may consider this a bold claim, yet the information I share with you consists of all the tools I have used explicitly to create gains for myself.

As you page through the book, you will start to feel more confident in your investing knowledge, and feel empowered to pick up the pace and take the next steps.

The great news is that the final two chapters are all about action and passive income. You will have so much knowledge internalized, and now it's time to put it into action. I know that you may want to skip directly to chapter 8, but I urge you to take it step-by-step. Each chapter builds into one another, and without the investment knowledge covered in the previous sections, you will find it challenging to apply the plan set out for you. Yes, you did read that right - the plan is set out for you in detail, and all you need do is follow along and take action.

Following the plan and doing the work of investing will bring you the financial freedom you seek. Perhaps you've been browsing online and saw a young person sharing how they created financial freedom for themselves through investing. They talked about passive income and living the laptop lifestyle. You wondered how they did it?

You are not alone in wondering this. So many people wonder this, and life gets in the way. They get busy with college, work, and home responsibilities. Therefore the last chapter will bring everything you learned together and show you how to create passive income for your future. You'll learn exactly how to retire young, and financially free without relying on a retirement fund or a job till you're 65.

Yes, you guessed it; we'll be going deep into investing wisely and showing you the facts about creating passive income that will help you earn while you sleep.

You have built an exciting roadmap for your journey through investing. All that remains to be said is: "Where do I start?" That's a great question. The best way to start is with the first chapter, which lays out the fundamental ideas you'll need to start investing. The book is a progression of each chapter with one section leading to the next.

Getting the most from this entails your active participation in the action steps after every chapter. This vital step will ensure you make progress towards your investment goals.

Finally, always read with the end goal in mind, and your investment journey will be a fruitful one that will help you achieve financial freedom along the way. I'm so excited that you chose to take this investing journey, and I'm looking forward to your success stories and for you to be financially free soon. First, let's grab a coffee and get into "What is investing?"

II
Financial Freedom

This very question deters many people from finally taking that leap into investing.

What is investing?

You know you want to invest, and you've seen others do well at investing, yet somehow you cannot seem to pluck up the courage to do it. There seem to be too many touch points, and the learning curve does appear to be steep. It's only natural to have this feeling about learning a new skill like investing.

In this chapter, you will get a keen insight into the reality of investing and what it involves. You will experience examples where people have invested both time and money and how it brought them inevitable success.

If you consider that investing is not a new concept, you may start to see that there are many ways that people have been investing over the decades and even the centuries. As a starting point, investing can simply be to set aside some money so that you can use it in the future to give you some form of benefit.

In the investing world, this benefit is known as a return. Some investors choose to invest in real estate; others invest in stocks and then do so in the hopes of seeing a return on their investment.

In this book, I'll be sharing insights into how you can invest in the stock market to get benefits and, ultimately, a return on your investment. Before you start investing in the stock market, it's also good to know about the principle of investing and how it currently applies to your own life.

Let's consider a few types of investments right now in your life that bring you some value.

Investing in your vocation

Firstly let's talk about your future employment. You may be working towards reaching pinnacles of success in your chosen field. Many popular areas of study right now include business management, engineering, robotics, and medical degrees. Naturally, there are many, and you can view an extensive list here at CNBC.

Would you agree that lots of work, effort, and sacrifices are needed to reach your career goals?

Examples of work include doing more than the required work set out and going above the norm. If you're currently studying, some of your work could be waking up at 06 am every single day and getting an early study session before you have to head to your classes. You may also forego the luxury of hanging out after class in favor of studying at the library or talking to a lecturer about a challenging chapter in your textbook.

Another work aspect could be that you choose to sit right at the front of the class, and because you have read the textbook extensively, you quickly absorb the discussion and gain more from your lecture.

In terms of a job context, you may be new to your job, but even so, this is the best time to put your best foot forward. You decide that in 6 months you want to advance at work. To do so, you realize that work in the form of understanding the practical nature of your job, networking, and engaging with the top performers in your field is of the utmost importance. Yet while the hours are long, you know that you will gain a benefit over time in the form of promotion and extra pay.

Let's consider effort as something you could invest in. You could be taking the initiative in every aspect of your college career, including asking the right questions, building positive connections with other students, and your lecturers. And of course, sacrifices include staying in to study instead of attending college parties and events.

Yet, you can consider that before you arrived at colleges, you needed to make positive investments for your future. Any ambitious student knows the requirements needed to become an exemplary performer at the highest levels.

First, you had to study hard to get the right grades to gain entry to the college of your choice, and also you had to work part-time to save up for college if you did not get a scholarship. Even if you did get a scholarship, you had to do it with painstaking effort and sacrifice, such as limited-time hanging out with friends, declining fun events, and giving every ounce of energy to your goal. That considerable investment for a bigger purpose of getting a degree drove you towards these sacrifices and paid off massively.

Let's also consider that perhaps your parents had to set aside money in savings and investments to send you to the best private schools and even help you pay for college. Maybe they did this by investing money for you from a young age, and these funds matured and allowed you to go to college. This financial investment from your parents grew over time and helped you to reach your goal.

Then, you likely had to earn that money to finance your way through college through part-time work or summer jobs. It's clear the investment needed to make a success of the college is vast, but the outlook of positive returns makes it worthwhile.

In this section, a significant investment was required into your vocation or college career to get a benefit that will be far-reaching. You may not have seen the rewards during those initial years. Yet, you instinctively knew that the benefits would come into your life in the form of a scholarship, a graduate degree with honors, or becoming the next VP in your company.

Investing time in your leisure activities

Moving along to making a success of the college, imagine that you get your dream job, or you make it into graduate school. This step is a considerable achievement, and you should be proud. And you know that's where the real work truly begins, and you strive to get to the top and reach the highest summits of success. Yet working all the time is simply not healthy for your physical and mental outlook for life. I know that many professionals say you should be working 24/7, but the reality is that everyone needs to take a break. Your mind and body need to recuperate. Studies are increasingly showing that balance is key to performing at your best in all areas of life. Recent research by the Harvard Business School indicates that 94% of employees spend 50 or more hours working.

And while you may think long hours are vital to getting ahead, you may have noticed a shift towards more work-life balance that will help promote well-being. There are more opportunities these days to take a break and do the things you love. You find that working extensively is beneficial, but investing in your time will bring you better productivity, more work-life balance, and sustained energy over time. Yet, you must embrace the act of spending time doing things you enjoy with the people in your life to gain the long term benefits fully.

Speaking to this information, you must seriously consider doing something for yourself to perform at your peak. A good bet would be to introduce recreation and fun into your lifestyle. Examples of relaxation could be taking a vacation, going to the movies, going hiking, and even going to an amusement park for a couple of hours.

Let's consider that you decide to invest in yourself and see the latest blockbuster at the cinema. It's the new and exciting superhero movie that everyone has seen except you. This outing is excellent for you as you get to treat yourself and your loved ones to a fantastic day out. You also get to refresh and enjoy an activity, making you feel like you have recharged your batteries fully. Your family is also happy as you managed to spend quality time together and build a bond as your kids are growing up; you also contribute money towards this activity. Of course, the money was not a waste, and neither was the time. Your input of cash and time justified the benefits of rejuvenation, energy, and building great experiences with the people you love. Therefore time and money invested in conjunction provide you a positive and happier life.

While investing time in your studies and work provides you with the ultimate benefits for your future, so too does taking time to rest and recuperate. This is also an investment that gives you more renewed energy to do your work effectively and consistently.

Your investment portfolio

Perhaps you've tried your hand at investing before, and you now have amassed an appropriately sized portfolio.

Or perhaps you have not heard of a portfolio before. Let's discuss this briefly, so you have a better sense of this aspect for the chapters to come. A portfolio is usually held by investors or managed directly by financial professionals. In a portfolio, you will find all the investments you've accrued over time.

Here are some critical examples of potential investments that could be in there:

Financial assets: This includes company stocks, bonds, and cash equivalents
Nonpublic traded securities: This would include real estate or art.

So as an investor, you would aim to get a financial return by mixing these assets to achieve an income long term. In this book, I'll be sharing my experiences investing in the stock market, and you will learn more about how to diversify your portfolio with well-performing stocks in later chapters.

Usually, If you have reached this stage of investment and have an essential portfolio, you may have progressed ahead, yet you don't quite grasp all of the intricate details just yet. In other words, your portfolio will give you positive returns in the long term, perhaps 10, 15, or 20 years from now. Let's take this one step further; your investment portfolio may have started with a small round of stocks recommended to you by your financial advisor at your bank. Alternatively, your parents helped you to find this lucrative investment opportunity, and you took their advice and took action.

Or you may have read multiple books on investment and figured it out all on your own. That is the more challenging yet very fulfilling way to get started too. The fact remains is that you now have an investment portfolio that you started building some time ago. In this example, you would have invested time to engage with books, parents, financial advisors, and more to ensure you were making the best decision with your money.

Then you may have invested time to create funds to invest, and that time investment could have been while you work at your job or part-time job. Here again, time was a significant factor in creating this income. You could then leverage the time investment and create financial rewards to invest. Over time, you start to see the growth in your portfolio yield ten times the initial investment.

You may have observed that you need to make some form of investment in the way of time, money, focus, or attention.

Ideally, you would love to get time, money, and focus without the strain, yet it's simply not as fulfilling.

The biggest thing you should consider is that the goal here is to build your freedom through investment. Many entrepreneurs, professionals, and students often find that if they cannot invest money, then they have to clock in the time for maximum output.

Let's take studying for your MBA. You have to invest both time and money for you to gain an education. Yet, it may be costly at the moment, but you have to keep in mind that it will reward you in the long term. For example, if you're currently in graduate school, you hope to be a business executive someday or entrepreneur. Your investment of time and money will pay off when you apply for jobs at fortune 500 companies using the information you learned during your time studying.

Now, as an entrepreneur, the knowledge and connections you've built up will also set you in good stead to create your own business, which will yield unlimited financial rewards. In this scenario, it's key to understand that money will bring freedom. Suitable financial wealth allows you to do all the things you would love to do without checking if you will be able to afford it. It gives you options and halts all forms of obligation you may have to a job. Therefore your investment of time or money could be the prepping ground for your financial freedom.

You have a sense of the dynamics at play when it comes to freedom related to money and time. Let's consider a practical story that can help you contextualize the information suitably.

Let's take the scenario of John, who wanted to learn how to play the piano. As you would imagine, it was quite expensive for the lessons due to the financial challenges his parents faced. Yet it was his dream to play the piano. He loved the sounds and the movement of pianists. This enthusiasm brought him to the realization that he needed to do something that would make the difference. Even though he did not have the money, he knew he could provide value to people. So he decided that since he had a pretty good voice, he would sing at relatives' parties or events. And he asked his relatives if he did an excellent job then they could pay him. If not, he would not accept payment. The good news is that he ended up being a rather good singer and people were impressed. So he earned money over time and could pay for piano lessons.

You see, this allowed him the opportunity to invest money in his music lessons. It turns out that John was a talented musician and simply needed an instrument to channel his talent. Over time he mastered his craft and invested time and effort to do his best. Soon John had earned a scholarship to a prestigious music school Juilliard to study music. John eventually went on to participate in famous orchestras all over the world. And it started with a single investment of time and perseverance. This exciting story gives you clear distinctions where investing time gives you the power to start using your passion. Your passion soon turns into an income-generating aspect in your life that can grow and multiply into a lucrative pay-off.

Let's consider you, let's take a scenario where, just like John, you decided that you wanted to expand your horizons. You felt that you were leading a monotonous and dreary life at present. So you decide that you would like to start earning an income on the side. Perhaps you enjoy writing in your spare time, so you start writing half a page a day. Imagine by the end of the week you would have written three and ½ pages. Now, in a month that adds up to 15 pages. Soon, after one year, you will find that you have written a novel. Everything grows with time, patience, and consistent effort.

And the fact that you invested that time, regular efforts means you can enjoy the success of creating the novel. As a starting point, you can publish your book, and perhaps people will love what you wrote. This step means some form of fame and remuneration. Yet, let's consider that all that time spent writing has given you considerable experience, and your next book gets completed in half the time. Often you get the most unexpected benefits from investing.

Next, let's consider an investment in improving your physical health. Each year almost 50% more people join a gym in January than the rest of the year. And they hope to gain a six-pack, become more attractive to others and hopefully find a suitable partner. In the same vein, by the end of February, the gym is empty despite the large groups of people who signed up in January. Yet, interestingly enough, it does not last very long as studies show that 80% of the new members will quit within five months.

Consider that 14% of new gym-goers quit before the end of February. Even though this is great for gyms as they can get more business in January, it's not that grand for the members who quit. You see, they invest so much into the gym membership, some even having to commit a year's fee only to leave after a month. On the other end of the spectrum, we have the rest of the 20% who invested and saw some real rewards.

What happened here?

Hopeful people went to join the gym to meet their goal of fitness or weight loss. They invested money and the potential of time to reach their goal. 80% of the people who joined but quit ultimately lost their investment because they were not willing to give their time and patience as a form of investment to lose weight.

Alternatively, there were successful gym-goers. They decided to plan their gym attendance. They knew that if they invest $80-90 per month, it would mean that they need to commit fully. What would commitment look like for these success stories? If you consider that they need to form a habit of waking up early to start a workout every day, as well as change their diet - it means massive sacrifices. Yet, it's not impossible, and they knew that the secret was doing it consistently, even when it was challenging.

They achieved a reward for their investment because they followed through. On the other end of the spectrum, many others did invest time and money in the beginning, but because they stopped going, they ended up wasting all of that time and money. Sadly for gym goers who quit halfway, they did not take time to practice diligence and build good habits.

It's vital to understand that time and money is significant investments to help you improve your future. Yet, it's also about your consistency over time and your passion for getting results. Financial investing can be the start of something meaningful that will bring you financial freedom. And when you invest in life, stocks, or anything at all, you will find that the rewards build up gradually until they multiply without any sign of stopping.

Key takeaways

1. Investment does not always have to mean money. Financial investment is one form of finance, but there are many others. You learned that knowledge investment would help you earn an income.
2. Investments at times are slow to grow and require patience before they show you returns, and during that time, you should be consistent and aim to keep building that investment of time and effort.
3. There are a variety of different avenues to explore when investing, and if you have things other than money to spend - make sure you put yourself out there and connect with the right people.
4. Taking the initiative when investing is essential and you may not always have the right resources at your disposal. Therefore, you may need to trade time for money at that specific time.
5. Other investments include money, time, focus, and love.

Action steps

- Consider how you invest your time or money at present and write down three aspects of your life where you can make some form of investment.
- Look at the investments you make and decide whether you will gain some benefit in a few years from this investment.
- Review what sort of investment you would be willing to make if you knew that you would be able to have financial freedom and retire at a young age.

We started by sharing that you can invest in many ways. From the would-be pianist that sings at family gatherings to someone who wants a six-pack - each had a goal that needed time or money investment. And they found it necessary to think of unique ways to get what they want using what they have. As with you right now, perhaps you're new to the investing world or on the brink of completing your final year of college. Maybe you're in debt, and you think you cannot invest just yet. Or you could only be looking at a new avenue to generate a sizeable income,

The truth is that investing is not that far out of your reach if you're willing to be patient and use what you have at present to get ahead. As you're pondering what you can invest right now, it's a good idea to consider how you can first use your unique talents to improve your investing ability. This topic is what we'll explore in chapter two.

III
Investing

In many ways, the adage that investment in yourself will yield excellent results is accurate, especially now when the world seems quite uncertain. You're facing the most turbulent time in history, and the only sense of control you have is to focus on yourself and invest in your skills.

And of course, as time goes by, it remains ever prominent that you have to improve, get better with resources and create new synergies to keep evolving. And while you may be experiencing a devastating situation, the internet has made it so simple for you to learn everything. The fact that you are now reading this book shows that you are willing to make a substantial investment in growing your skills.

You went in-depth into investment in the previous chapter, and you made a note of some of your investments at present. This would have created some awareness of your current investments of time and money, and the work you did in the previous chapter will set you up to understand how to invest in yourself in this chapter.

Lesson topics

- To appreciate that there is a process to investment, and it takes time to see the results of investing truly.
- You must always think of how to invest in yourself first and how you can use that to your advantage
- To see reading as a critical instrument in broadening your knowledge base on investments.
- Practical tools to practice patience while learning the ropes of investment.

Contents

- Investment success
- Invest in yourself
- Why reading is the ultimate investment
- Takeaways
- Action steps

Investment success

Success in investment requires a critical consideration, which is in short supply. I'm talking about patience, of course. It's a reality that success takes time, work, and perseverance. This aspect is even more critical when considering financial investments.
There may be times that you invest and only see the rewards years later.

How will you handle the waiting?

And generally, if you don't let the impatience get to you, you will find that the wait allows you the time to improve incrementally in skills, knowledge, and other factors too.

Let's consider that investing in this chapter will be about investing in you.

Many other people will tell you that you should take care of yourself first and be the best version of yourself while you wait for success. That may be partly true because investing in yourself is a sure-fire way to keep you fit mentally and physically to take care of the challenges that come with success in investing.

To understand this concept more concretely, let's consider a graduate student who wants to become an Artificial Intelligence (AI) programmer for a large corporation like Microsoft, Facebook, or Tesla. This student had dreamed from a young age that somehow they would make a difference. They were always fascinated by technology and how it made people's lives easier. The student even built their own AI prototype while growing up.

The only investment the student could make was to use their proactivity to the best of their ability. They took it upon themself to find out everything there was to know about artificial intelligence, often using social media to find experts and following the conversation online. In this way, they could understand what was happening in a field that they loved. Since it was challenging to buy new books, they took out a library membership and borrowed books. They also read autobiographies from Elon Musk, Bill Gates, and others to understand the lessons from successful people.

They were fascinated by scientific papers as well as learning programming languages, so they registered on free websites like FreeCodeCamp to improve their coding skills. You see, in this scenario, the student was preparing for their ultimate goal of becoming an AI programmer through investment in knowledge. And all they did was invest time because the internet has made learning a whole lot easier and faster and its inexpensive having a library card to borrow books.

This person used ingenuity and creativity to unleash all the knowledge that was in the world. This example shows a persistent student with a plan for success. Intuitively, you can feel that this person is moving in the right direction towards their goals. They are investing all the inputs to make that goal a reality. Yet, let's consider how this could apply to your situation.

Perhaps you are currently studying, and your income is limited as well as your investing skill. Therefore, you must consider other avenues to increase your skills to improve your financial investing skills.

Let's play this out as we did with the example about the student. Imagine for a moment that you may not have the financial backing to invest just yet, but you do have 3-4 hours to spend working on your investing skills.

You could start by searching online for advice from seasoned investors, and there are many valuable sites such as advice from the greats like Warren Buffet, and as well as online information from NerdWallet. Alternatively, you may be more interested in people who are currently investing wisely and offering practical steps. The perfect spots would be forums such as the investing subreddit or the value investors. And while these are great tools, the information is scattered, so you find yourself confused.

You think to yourself: "I need a guide." And somehow you decide that a book will help you. And you may be surprised to find that many investors followed a similar pathway to get into investing.

Therefore in this chapter, I want you to consider how to invest in yourself for future success and wealth.

Invest in yourself

Let's consider a few opportunities for self-investment and how you can practically apply this in your own life for maximum benefit. As a starting point, people often underestimate the value of a good book. Yes, it may cost you a small investment of money, but the lessons are endless. By reading a book, you are absorbing the knowledge that 1000's of wiser people shared before you. People who wrote these books have the sole purpose of sharing their knowledge, helping others on the journey towards success because they know how challenging it can be.

Perhaps you're someone who buys a book excitedly, yet it lays around for months on end because you have found better things to do. The reality is that in the early stages of a book, it can take some time to get into it, but over time and if you read consistently, you will find that the contents of the chapters help you with challenges you may be facing at that time.

A great book can be read in various ways, either using the physical book or the eBook. The value of an eBook is that you can learn lessons wherever you go. The art of reading helps you build a vast fountain of knowledge showing you tips, guidelines, and also holding within it a mentor in your pocket.

This type of investment is seriously underrated. Books teach you things you will never learn at university. You will soon find that the more books you end up reading, the more connections you can make. The reality is that before you become a successful investor, you need to master yourself.

A good starting book to put your mind into a growth mindset is to read a classic book called 21 Habits of Successful People by Steven Covey. This book is still so relevant two decades after it's release. It gives you a road map to planning your life, improving yourself, and making continual improvements for success. While there are many more books, the goal is to start, and more books will find their way into your life. Surprisingly, you will find that these books are what you need.

Here is a list of 4 successful entrepreneurs and their reading patterns:

- Warren buffet spends 5-6 hours reading financial news
- Bill Gates reads a book a week which equates to around 50 books a year
- Mark Cuban reads for 3 hours every day
- Elon Musk humorously said he learned how to build rockets by reading books.

As a departing point one of the most successful investors, warren buffet summarizes his reading habits as follows:

"That's how knowledge works. It builds up, like compound interest. All of you can do it, but I guarantee not many of you will do it."

And the beauty of what he relays is that he is confident that many will choose not to read. This anecdote suggests that it is a tough challenge to learn so much, but if you are willing to commit, you could ultimately find yourself making the most unbelievable deals.

As an aside, an excellent way to read more books is to employ creativity in your approach to reading.

Here are smart ways to read more efficiently:

1. Read using Audible while you run on the treadmill - this is important as you can kill two birds with one stone. You can get a good workout while listening to your favorite books too. The only thing is not to get distracted by the book and miss your step. If you choose to exercise outside, you can also run with a healthy dose of your books intact.
2. Several apps are helping you to read faster. A good one is called Blinkist, which enables you to learn more quickly by summarizing popular books and giving you the critical take-outs for your messaging. This approach saves you the hassle from reading every single page, and you can consume about 2-3 books a day.
3. Learning how to speed read will shave off so much time of reading. You can find an excellent resource here, which gives you detailed steps in reading at double pace and also with maximum comprehension.

Why reading is the ultimate investment

The steps highlighted for you will help you understand the rewards that you gain access to when reading the right books. This framework will motivate you to increase your reading investment.

1. You buy a book and decide that you will read this book. In a sense, you're making the first commitment. Taking that first step invests money into the act of reading, setting you up to gain vital knowledge to ensure personal growth over time. This step is your first step into investing without getting any initial tangible rewards just yet.
2. And with any new book, no matter how appealing it is, it takes some diligence to read consistently, and you have to force yourself to focus. In this stage, you're excited about reading, but you now need to prioritize your time to invest in this activity. This second form of investment is time.
3. Your effort when reading this book is directly related to what you will get out of reading the book. For example, if you read a productivity book but don't apply the tools, you will find that your levels of productivity stay the same. On the other hand, if you diligently use the tools, then you will see massive gains in your productivity at work or school. This process leads to improved work ethic and even better job prospects. Your investment then becomes your work ethic, and your reward is confidence and more opportunities.
4. Let's consider how you can get something from your investment in knowledge. Consider that you will have a broader framework of knowledge available to you. You can limit your time spent on specific tasks because others have done it before you and shown you the way. Consider how

you can now engage with more high-value clients due to the knowledge you possess.
5. Overall, you have achieved a high return on your investment when you look at the fact that a $15 book has provided you so much value in terms of knowledge, skills, and experience.

A client I worked with recently gave me some valuable feedback about a book she read called Mastery by Robert Greene. She tells about how this book provided her with unique insights into mastering a subject. At first, she felt challenged in a new role at work. You see, she had just received a promotion, and now she was simply finding her feet. But her manager expected her to know everything. Initially, she picked up the book to get her mind off things, but soon she was gripped from start to finish. She ended up reading the 250-page book in a week. Her mind felt great, and she was ready to start improving.

She found that the advice and studies that the author brought to the fore gave her new insight into her work challenges, and suddenly she had a fresh take about handling her work challenges. Fast forward to 6 months, and she achieved the top manager award in her office. She set a goal so unattainable that she had to hit it.

We can see again how my client was able to make a small investment expecting very little from her reading adventure, only to find that it gave her months of pinpointed insights into her problem. She gleaned how to be a new manager and master her craft. She learned how to put in 10 000 hours to get the best results, and she also discovered how artists like Michelangelo and Mozart handled mastering their craft. She could apply those very lessons to her work.

In a fascinating study, 26% of American adults admit that they have not read even a part of a book this year. And additionally, people who read books are said to live longer according to a recent study by Yale researchers. This new study relates the finding that reading books help improve your cognitive health. You will find that you have a more extensive vocabulary, thinking skills, and overall focus. Combined with increased emotional intelligence - you can certainly see the merits of reading actively as an investment for your life.

Looking back at our story about the new manager earlier, it may be clear to you that her success was a result of her direct investment in learning, reading, and growing. She made the right investment. She knew that time and energy invested now would yield adequate results later.

Before we move forward, reading is undoubtedly an excellent investment that provides you extensive knowledge and skill rewards. There are, of course, other ways to invest in yourself, such as getting a mentor, as well as furthering your education and taking a course designed to improve your skills. While we have not included those types of investments in this chapter, it's always a good idea to have those options too.

I'd like to touch on one other point where you could certainly invest in yourself. This is a point that distinguishes the successful investors who create lifelong wealth versus the unsuccessful investors that do not seem to get anywhere. Yes, I'm talking about investing in good habits for your life. In later chapters, I'll be sharing my unique practices of investing and proactivity. Yet, it did take me time to build that habit.

Consider how you can improve your discipline, whether it comes to waking up earlier or putting aside money every month. This is a way to delay your gratification so you can achieve rewards at a later stage. Remember if you are saving money, then you are foregoing different rewards like going to a music festival or buying an expensive new shirt. While you may get benefits from those aspects in terms of fun and pride, you will lose out on saving funds that you can use to invest in the future. Yet, it's a challenge for most people, since everyone loves spontaneity and variety in how they live their life. I can tell you though that soon the fun wears out and you will wish that you created good habits early.

In his now hugely successful book, Atomic Habits, James Clear highlights that you must slowly build good habits like taking mini-steps towards saving. This is how I created my investment habits too. It was challenging at first, but over time and with incremental growth, I found that my savings habit grew with time. I would say that even investing $100 each time was helping me build up the investing momentum, and I soon turned that into $1000 and so forth. Therefore, learning good habits early on in the game is a good rule to add to your arsenal.

Key takeaways

1. As a first time investor, consider that you must invest in your skills and knowledge base before reaching into your pockets to invest money into the real world.
2. There are hundreds of opportunities to invest in yourself, and all it takes is a little initiative from your side to uncover these tools.

3. Investing in yourself is a journey and has many value-adding steps that bring you success.
4. Learning to invest and empowering yourself can be challenging at first, but with time and experience, you will improve. You may need to spend money at first, but soon the initial investment is far exceeded by your outcomes and improved skillset.
5. Investing in yourself is also about improving your discipline and building great habits earlier on. These habits will help you forego instant gratification in favor of long term benefits,

Action steps

- Think about some of the investments you're willing to make towards your dream about securing financial freedom. This could be time, love, or attention. Be creative.
- Consider two things you could do that could provide value in life and improve your investing knowledge.
- Choose two books that you will read over 60 days that will improve your knowledge.
- Make an effort to create discipline and good habits that will serve you well on your journey. Choose one practice that you would like to build over 21 days and work at it every day.

This chapter was an ode to investing in yourself so that you can gain sufficient knowledge and skills to be a good investor. In the absence of a substantial investment in yourself, you will simply be misguided on your road to becoming a successful investor. A specific rule of thumb is to consider that every new activity that will give you freedom needs time, money, or focus as an investment. Make sure you invest wisely in yourself so that you can be thoroughly informed as you enter the world of financial investments. Your mental stimulation is a large part of your ability to make informed choices about life, the future, and your business.

I urge you to look into this aspect as we embark on our investing journey to success; investing in your knowledge is a stepping stone to more significant and prolonged returns on your investments in the future. This process leads us to look at more tangible investments that you may consider now that you have a keen understanding of investing. These are vital concepts that will serve you well as I now take you through an essential aspect of investing, which is even more prevalent during the pandemic we face in society. You'll discover how you can use timing and even major global recessions to your advantage when seeking out the perfect investments for your portfolio.

IV
Self-Evaluation

It's quite interesting to observe the world right now, as panic and fear set in. Many people are quickly shrinking away from all forms of investment and following a low-risk approach. And it's fair, the COVID 19 pandemic brought on many challenges for so many economies and the world at large. Yet, there have been many crises the world has faced over time, such as the recession in 2008. This resulted in the collapse of the economy at a scale we had never seen before.

Interestingly enough, there have been 47 recessions in U.S. history, and the point I want to make is that many people struggled during and after the downturn. In contrast, others benefited extensively due to planning, thinking on their feet, and using timing to their advantage. Make no mistake; I'm certainly not a proponent of pandemics or wars, I'm sharing these aspects to give you a view of history and how investment can be made during the harshest of times. The old thinking says that you should stay on the safe side and take no risks, but a newer version is that you should keep your eye on the global economy at all times, and you can even make a good investment during times of a down market.

As they say in almost every aspect of life, timing is everything. The fact is that knowing when to invest is as important as knowing what to invest in. I've covered some ground in terms of investment and what it is and what it could mean for you. And indeed, you have received critical insights into the way forward, and that is to invest in yourself as a starting point but also to understand the intricate details needed to be a substantial investor.

That said, it's appropriate that we step into the best advice on the best time to invest. In this chapter, I have reliable information that will steer your investment mindset into a positive direction that will spur you forwards. Ultimately, by the end of this chapter, you will know when to get into the market and when to buy so you can make a profit.

Lesson topics

- Be constantly vigilant during recessions and pandemics so that you can make a substantial investment
- You will learn about the benefits of investing during a recession and a pandemic.
- Find supporting evidence that investing during global and U.S. economic downturns can help you buy good stocks at their lowest

Contents

1. Investing during a recession
2. Investing during a pandemic
3. When the global and U.S. economies are down
4. All-time lows and sell-offs

Let's get started by looking at investment during a recession.

Investing during a recession

The year was 2008, and naturally, the economy was sailing along. People were enjoying some of the best years in the U.S. economy. Yet something sudden and dramatic changed everyone's lives. And it will undoubtedly be remembered for a long time.

It was an economic downturn that had devastating effects on families, businesses, and the economy as a whole. People lost their jobs, and houses and shops were shut down with no hope of return. The only future that was available in people's hearts and minds was a bleak one. This was everything that people did not see coming, and it was creating a gloomy world with very little to look forward to. Ultimately things had gone bad very quickly.

Here's what happened that may help you understand how the economy works and how, even in a lousy economy, somehow, people still do thrive.

The great recession or the 2008 recession, as it's now known, was caused by so many variables—the most significant reason being the subprime mortgage crisis. Ultimately, people were given homes that they simply could not afford, so that the banks could profit from this.

In other words, the borrowers were at high risk, but their home loans were approved, but at a higher interest rate. Yet, it started way before that period, around about the mid-2000s, to be exact. Their prices of homes were rising, so mortgage lenders tried to maximize their profits during this rare period. They did this by broadening the criteria for lending. More people were approved for loans, and it created a positive outlook for the economy. But of course, it was short-lived when people started to default on their payments, producing a deficit in income. It reached a critical stage, where homes had to be repossessed. This caused many people to lose their homes and big mortgage broker companies to go bankrupt. It caused the U.S. economy to plummet and take the global economy along with it. The government had to do significant damage control in the form of a stimulus package. You may be seeing something similar happen with the current pandemic, whereby a stimulus package is being applied to help the economy and prevent a similar situation that occurred in 2008.

And this incident was an example that nobody wanted to repeat, but many investors benefited during this time:

Warren Buffet, who famously said, "Be fearful when others are greedy and be greedy when others are fearful."

He purchased $5 billion in Goldman Sachs shares, and also $3 billion in General Electric shares at a low-interest rate during this period. As a result, Buffett has made billions for himself but has also helped steer these and other American firms through a challenging period.

Another person who also benefited big from the recession in 2008 is Satoshi Nakomoto, who is associated with Bitcoin. It may be that he used an alias to create Bitcoin, yet nobody knows who he may be. His impact on global economics has been significant, becoming more influential as he aims to change the fabric of the monetary system. And he certainly is another example of how to leverage the timing of a situation for your gain.

Looking at the economy and how it can be exciting, yet when disaster strikes, it takes everyone by surprise. The sooner you recover and see the opportunity instead of focusing on the panic, you may find that you can come out of any recession now and in the future a little wiser and wealthier too.

Let's now talk about the current global pandemic we face.

Investment during a pandemic

Initially, when COVID-19 started to take flight in Asia, there was so much confusion around the impact in Jan 2020. It had just begun and was isolated in Wuhan province in China while I was soaking in the information via CNN and Fox news. It did not seem that it would reach the shores of the U.S., and I knew that previous issues of this nature were contained effectively. Yet, enter March 2020, and suddenly the virus had reached countries all over the world, including the U.S.

The forecasts that I had dismissed were starting to come to life. And right now, as of writing, the COVID-19 virus has significantly affected the U.S., the economy, and the people living here. There are strict lockdowns for nonessential people, and we're practically waiting for a time for life to get back to normal.

Even so, there was much panic and fear. As an investor, I knew the lessons from the past and could see the signs. I could see that while the economy was taking a knock, it also meant that high valued investments were reducing their prices to an all-time low. This meant an opportunity for a host of investors globally.

The first thing that you must keep in mind is that investing while there is a recession or pandemic will pay off, provided you do things the right way.

And as the world is a mess right now, you can quickly get saddled with stress and leave everything by the wayside. And that's what most people will do in fact. Yet, it would be the wrong move for your situation, especially if you have goals of retiring young and retiring early.

I want to discuss the idea of a recession that can bring home many rewards for a savvy investor.

A recession would be considered a low turn in an economy, especially when the economy was experiencing a peak over many years. At present, in 2020, you can certainly see that the U.S. was experiencing an excellent economy since the last recession, and indeed there seems to be some form of change happening that will impact the economy for years to come. In other words, it's an economic decline and brings in unemployment in mass fashion.

You may even start to see massive drops in the stock market while the housing market simmers and gets worse from there. Yet it's an interesting fact to know that the U.S. government can only name it a recession if the gross domestic product of the country has been in decline for six months or more. Yes, this may be bad for most parts of the business world but not for the savvy investor.

You may be tempted to think that investing during a recession is silly, considering that everyone else is being prudent. You should refrain from following the crowd in this way. Remember that the best way to make more income with your investments is to buy and hold them.

And I said earlier; timing is everything. The bad times are an opportunity for you to get incredibly low prices on other stocks, and that will rise when the recession winds down.

Like I said, going in with a sense of panic is sure to dull your thoughts and make you do things you will not thank yourself for later. Always be thinking about the future and how great your portfolio will look after the rough times have passed.

The good news is that if you learn to thrive and survive in a recession, you're equipping yourself for the next one. The reality you must face is that recessions are a constant of the economy, so you must learn to navigate the waters.

These are the best ideas to be a savvy investor during a recession:

- Since you understand the context of recessions and the basic definition and you also have some perspective now, remember that with every downward trend, there will likely be an upward one. So keep this in mind when investing during a recession. The market will reward you in a few years, and the sacrifice you made will pay off big time.
- You may also want to consider consumer staple environments like consumer goods like food items or commodities that are always needed and in short supply.
- Be engaged in the marketplace, read everything about companies and the stock exchange, and make well-informed decisions.

Overall these are a few ideas that will help you take advantage of a recession and use the resources and your ingenuity to create an opportunity for yourself. The good news is that if you continuously planned for such occasions, you would not need to beg, borrow, or steal to find the money to buy the low stock or investments.

If you have some cash that you are not using it, then the timing could not be more perfect for the money. The coronavirus pandemic has impacted the stock market. But it's also made many stocks better priced. More than they've been in quite a while.

If you are wondering how you should invest your cash, then I'll be taking you through this in detail in later chapters.

To give you a taste of why time is so essential, here are a few ideas to set you on the path to investing when the timing is just right.

If you're in the market for safe, steady investment during these turbulent times, you will find that there many options to choose from. And many companies have been offering extreme discounts to get rid of the stock. This opportunity is all due to the surprise attack that COVID-19 brought to the fore. There's no more suitable time than this moment to grow your portfolio extensively.

An excellent place to look is in the medical sector. These are aspects needed the world over, especially when it comes to medications that need to be taken regularly. Therefore, and as you would imagine, healthcare companies are reaping the benefits of this. And you can, too, if you buy stocks at places like GlaxoSmithKline. They are currently experiencing a ten year low, and you can get a dividend of up to 5.8%.

Next up is Abbvie. They can boast about rather high dividends, and you can get a yield of up to 5.9%, they hold a top-selling inflammatory treatment known as Humira.

Also, consider Bristol Myers Squibb. While it only gives a yield of 3.5%, yet it's great because you can purchase it for a low price and achieve the necessary gains along the way. There is enormous potential for this company in the future. Their top-selling drugs are Opdivo and Eliquis.

And of course, you would know all about Pfizer. Interestingly enough, Pfizer has been struggling with revenue growth for a few years and can offer a 4.3% dividend yield. They are generating a few changes, and it might be worthwhile to give them a shot, as the transformation looks to be massive.

Taking advantage of a situation to gain financially is not strange. People have been doing it for centuries and will do so for the next few centuries too. Yet, the good news is that you are looking at data and being sensitive to the tides of the economy.

This sensitivity will pay off. Consider that the COVID-19 pandemic has caused mass challenges globally. It's unprecedented that an epidemic could affect the entire world in such a short space of time.

Nobody saw it coming, and indeed, it was not something that economists, leaders, or business owners thought to add to their financial plan. It's the right time to put on your investment cap, and start thinking about solutions to the current problems.

If you did save up and have sufficient funds available, this would be the best use of your funds that will grow into exponential amounts of money.

That being said, let's move forward to a discussion around how the plunging Dow can be beneficial to you.

All-time lows and sell-off

There may be a time in the market where stocks hit an all-time low and are being rapidly purchased by smart investors. Often these investors have been waiting for the prices to drop so significantly. And usually, you would only find out after the fact.

Why is this?

The simple answer is that proactivity is always crucial when understanding aspects like the Dow exchange and plunging stocks. Let's consider the Dow and then how you can take advantage of this tool in your investment journey.

The Dow is short for the Dow Jones Industrial average. It's an index that's used to give you an idea about the stock performance of a group of companies that are listed on stock exchanges in the U.S. It's a vital piece of information that investors use in their research and when deciding to buy a stock or not.

This is often the one that has been in the news lately and often creates irate investors or buyers. Yet it can be quite volatile at present.

During this time, companies are looking to sell instead of losing their entire company, and as an investor, you can pick these stocks up relatively cheaply.

This is what will move the Dow price:

Economic events: This could be a recession or a pandemic, as mentioned. Also, it could result from trade wars, most notably US-china trade wars.

Strength of the U.S. dollar: Naturally, a weak dollar will impact the index and the value drops, and may be appropriate to get your hands on some of the available stocks.

Government aid: Usually, a stimulus package or help will move the Dow index, and it may prove beneficial to move before the package takes effect and increases the Dow.

While it's great to know the impact, these ideas relating to the Dow is a great way to understand signs that the Dow is low, and it may be opportune to look at the critical investments that will grow over the years. It's also important to keep in mind that you should move before the economy fixes itself. Failure to do so will mean you have to wait for the next instability that will affect the economy and the price of stocks.

As you know, the recession in 2008 hit many people quite hard, and they are feeling the impact. It's been almost 12 years, and COVID 19 is creating the potential for recession once more. Yet, I wanted to show you that as a student of investing while young, you must stay optimistic during this time and plan accordingly to avoid the impact this will have on you.

Key takeaways

- We've seen recessions over the decades, and one of the more recent ones that devastated the economy was in 2008. The lesson here for you is that you can, and you should invest during a recession. This will ensure you get the lowest prices that will see an uptick in a few short years. Patience will be essential.
- Thinking about this aspect, know that the best time to start investing is when there is a major crisis like a recession or pandemic. Everything will be on sale, and you can take advantage of this situation.
- Understand the signs of a potential recession that will hit the economy such as the COVID-19 pandemic at present, and make plans to buy stocks or always have surplus savings or cash to take advantage of the downturns of the economy
- There will be all-time lows, and businesses will aim to sell off their stocks, especially in the DOW exchange. You just look out for this by keeping up to date on financial publications like investors.com and Financial Times. Consider setting up alerts that will keep you in the know so you can make your big move.

Action steps

- Be aware of the current financial news. Sign yourself up for Yahoo news, Financial Mail, and follow Twitter accounts to get a sense of what's happening in the economy.
- Look at the previous recessions with curiosity and think of how it can apply to the current pandemic.

- Make a list of good companies that may have experienced a dip in their stock price, but look set to increase shortly.

This chapter was undoubtedly filled with history lessons, and interesting economic downturns that investors the world over were taking advantage of. You learned that the economy fluctuates, and you should also be ready to move with it. I would reckon this is one of the most valuable lessons I've had in my time investing. I genuinely hope you have learned from this.

Let's now make our way towards the exciting world of where to invest for the best gains. This is the entryway into how you start your investment journey and will finally give you the best places to start. I'm sure you must be excited to get started and finding the investments that I discussed, so let's get into it in the next chapter.

IV
Timeline

I want to start by telling you a story about a little known bookseller that set out to create a better reading experience than Barnes and Noble about 26 years ago. You have to realize that at this time, Barnes and Noble was a giant in the bookstore industry, and they were the word on how to buy books, and reading trends and even had movies featuring them. Yet, this was the '90s, and things sure have changed, for the better! Remember the bookstore. Perhaps you've heard of Amazon?

Amazon started as a little known bookseller in the garage of Jeff Bezos's house. You can imagine the cool and sophisticated Jeff Bezos, who we regularly see on the news these days, working behind a huge PC in his little bookstore. At the time, he had recently quit his well-paid job to start an internet company. That was practically unheard of in the '90s, and those who did were often considered slightly strange. Now, of course, every second person you meet is an entrepreneur.

Flash forward to 26 years later of this story, and you have someone who is the wealthiest person in the world and whose company is giving investors something to be ecstatic about.

Amazon's star continues to shine, and in the early stages, its shares were selling at $23.50 in 1997. Let's fast forward to 2020, where the price of Amazon shares sits in the range of $2319. You can imagine that the investors in Amazon shares have been very pleased with their initial investment. The big jump is mainly due to time passing, and smart investments and integrations on Amazon's part.

And what a fantastic success story Amazon continues to be for investors. Therefore, in this chapter, I want to talk about where you should start your investment journey.

You will learn

- The four places that are great to get started on your investment journey
- An alternative to the brokerages suggests that it will help automate your investment process.
- Introduction to intrinsic value companies

Contents

- Stock brokerages
- Robinhood
- TD Ameritrade
- Merrill Edge
- Invest in companies with an intrinsic value
- Key takeaways

I started this chapter with a story of Amazon because, to me, it represents a success story of note, and shows how time can genuinely increase the value of a company. I want to share companies like Amazon with you to give you an indication of good companies that you should look out for when investing. In this way, the more you start to learn about good companies, you get insight into the characteristics that make them good and start looking at all companies in this way.

And who knows, if you watch closely and look at the advice shared, you may find the next Amazon that you can invest in too.

Yet how do you go about finding these companies?

I'm often asked this question, and my journey investing has been an excellent helping hand here. To be quite frank, when I started, there were not so many options as there is now. You had to be creative, curious, and willing to work to find these investments. I like that approach, but I do feel that I can make your life much easier by sharing the most efficient ways to find these companies.

There are many places that I've personally used to invest and achieve high rewards from, but there isn't a reliable directory that helps you find the right opportunities. This is the stop sign where most new investors simply stop looking. That would be a mistake that will cost you dearly.

You want to ensure that you are always on the lookout for the best investments that will give you positive yields over time, and this might be the best avenue to explore. That's why in this chapter, I will show you exactly where to look so you do not have to spend hours searching online or asking the wrong people and fall short of your investing goals.

In this section, my main point of reference will be to look at stock brokerages known as Robin Hood, TD Ameritrade, and automated brokers. I will then share details around what's needed to start and pro tips to help you make the most of these brokerages.

A brokerage is a great way to go when starting your investment journey as they offer you many stock options, and you can get started for relatively low upfront costs. Provided you've planned your finances correctly; your starting point can be a good one.

Definition alert - Think of a broker as someone or a firm that will charge you a fee (also known as a commission) for linking you up with investors who either want to buy or sell stocks or bonds.

In the past, a brokerage would have to be a brick and mortar environment where you could set up a meeting and speak directly with a broker. You may also need to feel like you have qualified with the right amount of money before engaging. I would imagine that most people felt intimidated to walk through those glass doors, and ended up not investing at all.

Luckily for us, things have changed dramatically. Those days are gone where you had to take paper statements around with you to make your investments, now it's all about doing it online, and in as little time as possible. You're busy, so it's best to use your time in the most effective way possible to find the right investment opportunities.

I'll share a few of these brokerage firms first, and then I'll offer you a more passive approach to selling and buying stocks or bonds for maximum effectiveness.

Robinhood

Robinhood was one of the first investment brokerages that offer commission-free investing, and can also help you funnel your money in the right direction. It helps your money work harder so that you don't have to.

How does it work?

- Firstly Robinhood is a brokerage firm that does not charge any commission fees.
- They aim to match you with the best investor or buyer so that you can get the best advantages of a stock or a bond.
- You don't need to have an account minimum, so it makes it supremely accessible for a range of investors with a variety of budgets. In other words, you have a partner who is committed to keeping investment costs low.
- You can expect to pay $75, which is for an outgoing account transfer fee, which is common and justified with most brokers. You use this feature when you need to transfer your investments to a new broker.
- They offer fractional shares, which means you can invest in a portion of stock to diversify your portfolio and genuinely build up while you are in the early stages of your investment journey.
- It's quite simple to use, and you can do it by using your smartphone. And you're likely quite savvy with your smartphone and can do many things like signing up within a few minutes as well as having an arrangement with banks they can process your application in about 1 hour. They do not need to validate your account by depositing an amount of money, and then awaiting your verification.

- The app is very streamlined, helping you to see all the aspects of your investment portfolios; you can also view your transactions, watch list, and account statements. You can also get details into each company and group them according to your unique needs.

Robinhood is a good starting point for your investing journey, the platform is available directly on your smartphone, and you can get started very quickly with little capital. You have many opportunities to test the waters as well as learn along the way. Perhaps you are considering a brokerage with more functions and features; then, you can take a look at TD Ameritrade.

TD Ameritrade

Following the same idea of 0% commissions, TD Ameritrade has proven to be a dependable brokerage firm with a good reputation too. They offer support to new and also seasoned investors who want to use the platform. Not only that, but their tools also provide excellent research opportunities so you can always make the best decisions.

How does it work?

- They offer you commission-free trades on stocks; Exchange Traded Funds(ETF's), and options trades. This means anyone can start on the platform.
- With a wide range of investment opportunities like futures, Forex, and Bitcoin - they leave a lot of room for a variety of investors to come on board.

- This is an ideal broker for beginner investors as you can start with $100 or less on a variety of mutual funds that have a high yield.
- The support is excellent, and they have an investment library of videos and resources that cater to all investment questions on their platform. Since they have such a vast range of data, they can share best practices.
- There are two platforms available for investors, namely their online website in the form of TDAmeritrade.com and then, of course, a more advanced platform called Thinkorswim, which is more for advanced users. These platforms give you complete access to your stocks, investments, and portfolios on your desktop.
- You may also invest directly via twitter direct messaging, Google assistance, FaceBook messenger. This is especially helpful when you cannot get to the desktop version of the site.
- Alternatively, you can also access the mobile version of the site, which is available for iOS users only. This is more for advanced users at present. Therefore, in the early stages I would stick with the leading desktop site for the best results.

Overall TD Ameritrade is a lucrative brokerage that stands heads and shoulders above most options, offering you 0% commissions while providing excellent service and opportunities for stocks and mutual funds too.

Of course, if the first two do not meet your needs, you can also check out Merrill Edge.

Merrill Edge

Bank of America's offering known as Merrill Edge for investments is a good option if you are likely just getting started. Generally, if you are a Bank of America customer, you do also get more benefits. They offer a truly integrated experience, especially when it comes to mobile use.

How does it work?

- It is a gateway between the investment opportunities and you, bringing well-sourced shares directly to your attention.
- You can do it online or choose to have a face to face conversation with a financial advisor.
- Gives you stock trades for free as do the other brokerages on the list. And also, it has a charge of 0.65 cents per contract.
- There are no annual or inactivity fees.
- Advanced features on mobiles help mimic a desktop view, so it feels like you're accessing the site on a desktop.
- They are renowned for thorough research and high-quality investment selection, and that's very helpful as a new investor.

Merrill Edge is a reliable online investment brokerage that gives you a lot of value when investing through your phone. Their rates are low, and also you have a wide variety of investments to choose from.

Let's move onto a more automated brokerage that will make investing even simpler.

Robo-advisors

These are called Robo-advisors, and while they may have the sound of a robot type broker who does all of the work, there may be some detail needed from you in this process. A Robo-advisor simply provides complete investment management, so you don't have to do the unnecessary admin associated.

Wealthfront is an excellent example of this type of broker. They offer solutions for new and old investors alike. And more importantly, they leave you with a hands-off approach to investing.

How does it work?

- It's an automated process whereby you fill in a questionnaire about your investment preferences. Once done, the platform does all of the work to give you the best investment suited to your case.
- Added to the previous point, it continues to manage and notify you of the stocks, so you are always kept up to date. The bonus is that you do not have to do much work in this process.
- It's backed by many reputable individuals who seek to support a more automated approach to investing while helping beginners along the way.
- Also, the investment combination includes a variety of stocks in the U.S as well as foreign stocks, emerging markets, and real estate too.
- They do charge a fee of 0.25% on the first $5000 of investment. That said, they offer a referral bonus if you bring your friends on board to the platform, and they invest.

Overall, Wealthfront is a new way to look at brokerages, and while they do have a fee, it does seem worth it considering you don't have to do the work of finding the best investments.

Looking at these starting points to start investing is all good and well, but you also need to learn how to choose the right investments.

In the next section, I want to share my experience on how to buy stocks and lucrative tips that have helped me over the last few years.

Invest in companies with an intrinsic value

Often this is in the eye of the investor. And there are many ways to calculate the intrinsic value of a stock. Over time I've learned that it can be a certain 'gut feeling' that goes along with this, yet you can also do due diligence by reviewing a few key aspects.

The first is that you take notice of brands or companies that are everywhere, as they seem to be spending significant amounts in marketing and can see the potential for growth in their company. Also, it's essential to consider that if you know a company with lots of visual presence - it means you may have been seeking it out and consider it a good brand. A good question to ask at this point is: "Would I buy this product?". If you have a resounding yes to that question, it may be worthwhile taking a look.

Here are a few good examples you may consider:

- Coca-cola
- Tesla

- Spirit Airlines
- Carnival cruises

Another critical factor that is often overlooked is that you must consider the future probability success of a company. This may take some work, but with a little extra research, you may find yourself a winner.

To illustrate this point, let's look at a company that continues to make bold moves in every way, and these have been paying off massively for its shareholders. The company is called Tesla. Their CEO Elon Musk is widely known for his efforts to push limits, and it's one of the reasons the company stays so competitive. Yet, if you consider Tesla when Elon bought the company in 2004, it was lacking capital. He had the money and decided to invest in the company. Yet, it only really started to gain some traction in 2010, and still, during that time, the stocks were priced at a low rate. Initially, 13 million shares of common stock were issued to the public for US$17.00 per share.

At this time, the price of Tesla stock is currently valued at $761.19. That's a massive jump up from the early stages, and investors may be very excited by the gains they have made.

As you would imagine, you should always choose the companies you invest it wisely, it could mean an exponential increase in your initial investment as indicated by the Amazon and Tesla Story.

Here are some essential factors when choosing the right company to invest in?

Look at the profit margin: This number is freely available for public traded companies, and you can also go ahead and compare it with companies performing well at the time.

Look at the return on assets: Remember that assets are anything that a company owns that has value when sold. When calculating this figure, remember the higher the number is, the better. You must consider these aspects, and most public traded companies will have this freely available in their annual reports.

Knowing this growth factor will show you companies that have a high probability of succeeding.

And while I'm sharing best practice, I also want to share a word of warning about **penny stocks** with you.

Penny stocks are commonly traded stocks of small companies, and they start trading at meager prices. Many investors buy them in the hopes of seeing massive rewards. It's often far from the case.

The main challenge with investing in penny stocks is that it is not easy to convert your investment into cash. This is due to the buyer and seller prices varying so dramatically - you often find it hard to reach a price point.

The second aspect is that penny stocks are extremely volatile, and they certainly fluctuate a lot more than other stocks. You cannot manage the stocks as effectively, and there have been countless people who have either won big or lost big. In other words, my advice is to focus on the different options I recommend in this book instead.

Overall, I can confidently say that if you follow the channels, I have provided you in this section and use it effectively, you will win at starting your journey into sound investing. Go ahead and check out Robinhood, TD Ameritrade, or Merrill Edge and sign up. It should take you less than 45 minutes to get set up and start investing.

Here's what you need to sign up:

- A stable internet connection
- Your first $1000 available in an account and ready to use on the site
- About 45 minutes and some patience

You can tell it does take minimal efforts on your part for high rewards, and the ultimate convenience is rather exciting, too, as you can simply work from your laptop or smartphone to get the ball rolling.

In other words, it's now become the most relaxed time in history to invest.

Key takeaways

- It pays to remember that investing with a stock brokerage will have positive yields that will ensure you always can sustain your portfolio's level of performance. Overall it's an excellent way to get started as brokerages know precisely which stocks perform the best. You may need to check around for the best brokerage, but the options I shared with you may be more than suitable to get you going.

- Also, consider that investing in great companies that have intrinsic value could be your best bet. These companies are solid shapers of suitable investments as they consistently perform well on the market and have a great brand as well. Keep in mind that you must do your homework appropriately and do due diligence before buying.
- Knowing where to invest is an exhilarating road that will help you discover so many essential aspects of larger-scale companies, and help you to leverage their name for your profit and purposes.

Action Steps

- Get into action by choosing one or two of the brokerages I listed here and sign up for their sites or download the apps.
- From here, most will want to integrate and connect your bank, so go ahead and allow that.
- Once done, you then have access to all the available investments and research about the companies.
- Spend 10-15 minutes a day on researching and understanding the platforms, and soon you will know it like the back of your hand.

This has been an exciting foray into the depths of where to invest for the best gains. I started by telling you a story about Amazon and how they rose to extravagant heights and took their shareholders along for the ride. It goes to show that once you understand the signs of an intrinsic value company and how to leverage these companies using tools like brokerages, you too can find lucrative investments in the likes of Amazon or Tesla.

These companies tell you an incredible story of how little companies can grow exponentially with patience and time. And as these companies grow over time, they also make your relative stock investments grow too. It's genuinely about knowing where to invest and choosing the right companies, tools, and avenues that will help you along the way.

You'll be pleased to know that in the next chapter, I'll show you the exact steps on how to win your investment. You can take a break or follow me over to learn how to win your investment.

66

V
Location

Starting my journey as an investor wasn't always an easy path, and it took me some time to find my feet and get proficient. I want to share that with you so you can get a clearer picture that the path to being a good investor that sees return has many learning curves along the way. I would say that every day brings something new to the table, and upsets the rhythm of the market. The one thing I've realized over time is that the market ebbs and flows, and that's the nature of it, so you have to be always on the lookout for opportunities to make the best investment.

You may find that a stock doesn't always look like it could reach the highest heights when you look at it superficially, or the data you acquired via your brokerages showed it was not the best option. Still, I urge you to look much more in-depth and see the details surrounding that investment and that company. That said, it's great that you are thinking about the idea of winning your investment.

You may want to stop and take a look at how far you've come. Did you know you could make such progress in investing within such a short space of time?

I'm reminded of a powerful quote by Jim Rohn, which sticks with me:

"Make measurable progress in a reasonable time."

It's really and truly about making progress slowly and steadily in your investment journey and keep going even if you cannot see direct results yet.

As for now, you come a long way. You've set your sight on the big league of investing, and with some fundamental knowledge, you know what investing is as well as how to invest in yourself for added benefits. And to add to that, you also know that a pandemic such as COVID-19 or a big recession as experienced in 2008 could bring new opportunities into your investing world. And knowing this has allowed you to step right into the enormous opportunities available for new investors right now.

The online space has made it extremely easy to start an investment account and get into the action in under an hour or less. Yet, it's still important to remember that you must be aware of your investment portfolio, your fund availability, but also the market at large.

This will help you realize the benefits of your investments over 10 or 15 years. I always consider an essential factor when investing, and I think about what the investment could be in the future. I look at it from all angles and take in all of the data available to me and finally make the decision to move ahead.

It's time to learn about the evolution of your investment and sealing the deal to win your investment officially.

Lesson topics

- The definition of a strategy known as "Buy low and sell high" and how to make use of it in your investment deals
- You will be shown the data around two companies that showed positive progression over 10 and 20 years
- How to use the strategies of buying low and selling stocks at a higher price later down the line
- Aspects to consider when using the "Buy low and sell high" strategy

Contents

- What does it mean to "Buy low and sell high"?
- Costco
- NVIDIA
- How to implement "buy low, sell high."
- Benefits and considerations of buying low and selling high
- Key takeaways

What does it mean to "Buy low and sell high"?

I thought for some time about how I would introduce you to this strategy which I use significantly when I'm investing. Therefore I've decided to kick things off with a scenario that will channel our thinking in the right direction.

Let's look at a potential investor who decided to buy stocks ten years ago with Netflix, which was selling at $13.01 in May of 2010. It was trading at a reasonable rate, and Netflix was starting its ascent into the stratosphere. You would remember that it was a streaming service that very few people knew about, yet it was gaining traction quite rapidly. And at the time, if our investor decided to buy stocks for $1000, they would have a total of 77 shares. And if you look at the current stock price, it's at $428.15. So right now in 2020, their $1000 investment is at $32,934 over ten years. I'd say they made a pretty good decision investing in Netflix. The simple scenario shows that looking at a company like Netflix in its infancy and purchasing a stock earlier on in the game can bring in many vital rewards down the line. The fact is that good companies are always growing. While Netflix may have started as a simple service offering independent movies, it soon turned into a company that produces the biggest shows attracting A-list stars to their company. And during COVID-19, they've stood heads and shoulder above other companies as they have provided a means to entertain people. You would agree they have all the makings of an intrinsic value company.

I want you to start reaching your mind forward to think about how your next $1000 could become 10x that amount and what that could mean for you. Instead of working till the ripe age of 65, you could take ten types of companies just like Netflix, invest heavily in them earlier on and see your investment multiply tenfold. The most crucial part is that you will be able to see this progression in 10 or 15 years, and it could help you sell and move onto financial freedom and living the life of your dreams.

Let's take a look at more details around buying low and selling high to solidify this strategy and make it even more practical truly.

While the adage "buy low, sell high" may seem easy enough and intuitive, there are a lot of factors at play. The first crucial distinction is to note that stocks fluctuate and are cyclical too. This means that they move up and down at their very own pace, and are impacted by world events(Covid-19), economic changes and perceived risk (think of how Elon Musk often announces details about his stock on twitter, and it has the power to change the price).

So you can probably see that the supply and demand influences of stocks are healthy. And naturally, this will influence the price. Yet the beauty of the buy low, sell high lies in this very principle.

So it's all about timing, as I mentioned in chapter 3. The idea is that you want to consider the lowest price that the share will go to and make a decision to buy at that point. At the same time, it does take some urging and decision-making ability to choose that exact point. Many investors have this challenge; they hope that it will go down even lower and wait and wait only to find that it skyrockets the next few days, and they acted too late. That's also something you should take into consideration when watching a stock on Robinhood or TD Ameritrade.

And conversely, you want to find the highest price the stock reaches and make it your mission to sell as soon as possible. You can see how the factors of buying and selling play off against each other. And you will find that you understand the market trends as you learn more about investments and start making your first few deals. Eventually, you will know precisely the right time to sell your stock for the most significant impact on your portfolio.

Yet if you do it well enough, you'll find yourself reaping the rewards.

Now that you have a good understanding of the "Buy low and sell high" strategy, let's look at a few examples of companies that show the trajectories that have over their lifetime increased significantly. This section aims to show you what to look for in the early stages of buying a stock as well as to help you analyze the stocks.

In each of these examples, I simply found data stock trends on Google, which are quite reliable and trended the data for the lifetime of the company involved. A quick how-to is that you take the stock you are considering and input this into Google, and the first search result will bring up a trended graph.

The graph also has a touch point so you can get the exact figure at the specific date you are looking at.

Let's begin by looking at Costco.

Costco

Costco is a company that sells wholesale goods, and over the last 10-20 years, they have seen massive gains in their stock price. Let's consider that in May 2000, their stock price was $52.78, and by May 2010, the stocks had shot up to $65.05. Yet the best change has been the next 20 years, where we see that Costco is currently at $317.92.

There has been a massive shift in consuming wholesale goods, and of course, during Covid-19, bulk buy has become essential. That's the reason you see such an enormous jump in the price. If you bought a Costco stock ten years ago, you would be delighted with your return. Similarly, consider if Costco's share will continue to rise the way Amazon shares have done and what it will increase in time.

Think broadly about the service they provide, such as bulk buys, and the trends around staying at home and how much convenience this will bring to people. Look also at their investments and how they intend to expand their company. These could be critical indicators of further growth. To give you a few clues, Costco is leveraging ecommerce right now in a big way as they have shallow debt exposure too.

Let's consider a different industry in the second example.

NVIDIA

You may not have heard of Nvidia Corp, yet you may know of the products that use their technology. It's a technology company that supplies the gaming industry with the tech they need to keep building the latest in gaming technology for their insatiable fan base. They are the leaders in graphic processing units for the gaming industry and more recently mobile computing. As these industries have seen a massive uptick over the last 10-20 years, so too have the stocks of NVIDIA. In May 2000, their share was at $6.65, and flash forward ten years later to May 2010 - the stocks rose to $17.11. This was a close to a double increase. And right now, the stock is at a whopping $291.28. This is one stock to watch closely as it will continue to increase and be perfect for the buy low, sell high strategy. As I did with Costco, I want you to also consider the variables at play with NVIDIA. They are a hardware company that supports mobile computing as well as the gaming industry. This industry has been moving forward rapidly, but it's interesting to note that the user base is quite young, and their market penetration is still in its early phases. Remember that as the younger user base grows up, joins the workforce than their affordability rises, they will need more advanced gaming technology. So long as NVIDIA keeps evolving the offerings and investing in new technology, they will see their stock prices go up too. This company looks set to further increase its share prices, exactly like Costco. And yes, you will see their share prices follow a similar trajectory to other winners like Amazon and Tesla.

How to implement "buy low, sell high."

Seasoned investors employ a few criteria in their "buy low sell high" strategy, and you need to understand these before doing the same.

The first marker is that they look at the trends of stock currently, and also at unusual fluctuations over time. They want to consider dips as well and review the reasons for this. The key is to understand the reasons for the decline to ensure that they will not see the same with the stock.

They also consider the highs of a stock as it could mean that the stock will reach its height at this point, and it may prove futile buying this stock. This is often done with market research and truly understanding the content of each share. Alternatively, it means that it's time to sell.

More seasoned investors will look at moving averages to make their decision of when to buy or sell. This will help to tell you how a stock price has been performing over some time. You can use a 50-day to show you how the stock performed for a shorter period or make use of a 200-300 day average for more extended periods.

Let's now consider the benefits of this strategy.

Benefits and considerations of buying low and selling high

In my experience, I've noticed plenty of benefits to this approach. The first is during times of fear; you can get stocks at a reasonably inexpensive rate. And this will lead to increases once the market picks up again. It will be well worth it always to keep your ear to the ground and keep up to date with current news to know when there is potential to buy stocks at a low rate.

Naturally, the market will pick up with these stocks, and you will see a quick spike allowing you to sell at higher rates.

Just as there are benefits to the strategy, you must consider a few critical aspects that may cause concern and future challenges.

Always consider all the details about a stock you wish to invest in. Research widely and make sure you make a well-informed decision.

Also, try not to follow the crowd, as in when everyone is purchasing a stock - you may want to consult, but yes, make the final decision with all the facts available at your disposal. These are essential considerations that will help you in the long run.

There are many tools available to help you "Buy low and sell high." I, therefore, wanted to share my favorites with you so that you maximize your investment strategies.

Key takeaways

- Learning how to buy low is a fine art and skill that you must master, but it takes preparation and insight to get there. Naturally, if you're willing to be patient, you will find yourself holding the best stocks at the lowest prices, and you will only be waiting for that magical growth factor to settle in.
- And of course, you did not just buy stock to hold onto it for years and years. I'd say a reasonable time frame of 15 years is sufficient to sell out and make a safety net that will last for years to come.
- All in all, if you do these things and regularly apply it to your Buy and sell methodology, you will rinse and repeat the process over time.

Action steps

- Review the "Buy low and sell high" strategy and ensure you fully understand the implications
- Look at companies other than those I have mentioned in this chapter, and do the trending exercise I shared with you over ten years. Follow the journey of the companies and read about them online.
- Apply the knowledge you have about "Buy low and sell high," by looking at companies that could fit the criteria to buy low. Right now is the ideal time to do this as there are

so many profitable companies whose share prices have dipped due to the sudden pandemic.

I started this chapter looking at the vast journey you have taken so far on investing, and also with a story about a very successful company called Netflix. I used the example of an investor who decided to throw in $1000 and 10 years later found his value of shares rose enormously. Of course, there were practical ways I shared that will help you achieve the same level of success, and it is all about doing your research and finding those opportunities like Netflix that will help you win big. That said, let's take a giant step forward into becoming an investor for the long haul by leveraging patterns in history. This will be an even more practical chapter that will highlight more stocks that have seen an overall increase in value over time.

VI
Winners vs. Losers

I recall watching in awe as Steve Jobs made his commencement speech at Stanford in 2005. He has always been such an inspiration, and he truly built up the brand and legacy of Apple Inc. as you may know it today. Yet, you may also know the stories, as highlighted in movies about the legend. Apple did not precisely have a comfortable ride to success, and at one stage, Jobs was removed from the company.

Who could imagine that a little company in the 1980s that started in a garage could become the giant that it is today? And while Steve Jobs may have left us with a legacy and taught us so many lessons, he also ensured that innovation was top of mind for his company.

And the innovation keeps on going to this day, and some say that's the reason Apple stocks have shown improvement over ten years.

This chapter hopes to look at historical trends and long term benefits achieved by a variety of successful companies and how to use this information for your investments in the stock market.

Lesson topics

- Practical stories about successful companies that have seen extensive growth
- To appreciate the long term benefits from investing and switch your perspective to a long term approach when it comes to investing.
- How to look at trends and make sense of the data for investment purposes

Contents

- Introduction to long term investments and Apple
- Benefits of the long term investment
- The incredible success of Amazon
- Microsoft stocks and their journey through time
- Key takeaways
- Action steps

Introduction to long term investments and Apple

I did start this chapter with an exciting story about the Apple company, so now I want also to review some of the exact numbers.

Apple has seen massive growth over time, and at present, the company is on a high. Yet about 20 years ago in May, their stock was valued at $4.03. While ten years ago, in May, Apple's stock was valued at $34.62. And if you consider today in May 2020, the price has jumped up to a massive $289.17.

The primary reason is that Apple's brand has been exploding over the last 20 years, as they innovate and make the best products available.

They keep on expanding on their range, reimagining the world of mobile and keeping their customer's experience top of mind.

This is indicative of their share price. Many investors in Apple scored a big payout because they bought low 10 or 20 years ago and have been selling over the last few years.

Benefits of the long term investment

As you can tell, the advantages of holding stocks long term are many, and significantly impact the value over time.

Many investors employ a variety of strategies for the stocks and ultimately make a solid return on their investment. You may find that some investors are quite analytical in their approach, looking at the finer details in the market while other investors employ a more intuitive approach as they try to get a sense of the market sentiment.

The reality is that, whatever you choose to do, you will have to follow that pattern and certainly have a semblance of a plan for long term growth. This is a cautious person's game, and if risk aversion is right up your alley, then this is the way to go. The good news for you is that when you decide to hold stock for a long time, the benefits are many, while the drawbacks continue to be few.

Let's consider some of these benefits.

The first is that you don't get overly emotional about your investment. As you have confidence knowing and watching as the price of your stock rises and falls, and this is necessary for how the market works. You start to realize that every time you see a dip, it won't be for long, and it will go up again. It entirely removes that feeling of wanting to sell your stock when you see a poor showing during a decline in the percentage. This only serves you to make you a more resilient investor who thoroughly understands the market and is in for the proper long haul.

The next thing I want you to consider is that you ultimately see a profit due to the long term investment. Significant data is showing that stocks perform much better than your standard savings accounts and bonds. The difference is stark, as indicated by CNN, which shows that stocks give you an average rate of 10% return when compared to a variety of other investments, which are just under 3 percent. It's clear to see that stocks have a good track record of making money in the long term. Consider this last aspect is that the details CNN shares are an indication of the market since 1926, so it's close to 100 years.

And perhaps you will relate to a gloomy nature of monthly or yearly taxes, but it certainly does put a damper on your spirit and your hard work. When you invest long term in the stock market, you have a lower tax burden. The tax on investments is known as capital gains tax, therefore if you keep a stock for a year or more, you will be taxed up to 20%, but if you keep it a short term, you will be taxed as regular income tax of up to 37%. As you would imagine, it takes a large chunk of your investment, and the best bet is to go with the lesser evil, of course.

And finally, another beneficial aspect of long term stock investment is that most companies are strongly regulated by the US Securities and Exchange Commission (SEC). Therefore it's so easy for you to get information and research done on these companies for your peace of mind. It's always recommended you fact check everything before you invest, and it makes it all that easier for you.

These benefits, coupled with the data, speak life into your investment story in a big way.

The incredible success of Amazon

I want you to consider stock in detail, namely Amazon. Yes, we touch on this briefly in chapter 3, but now I want us to take a deep dive into Amazon stock and understand the enormous gains they have made over 20 years. I'm going into much detail as I want to ensure that you also take a detailed approach when on the path to your investment journey. These lessons will be of vital importance when you're using brokerages like Robinhood and TD Ameritrade to buy your first stocks.

Simply you should marvel at this spectacular success story. I consider the story one of the genuinely significant gains. And to think that Jeff Bezos left his comfortable job and slept in his car while trying to get his new book business off the ground. Bezos and the early founders used to pack the items on their own, and have these shipped off to customers. You can probably imagine a Bezos in 1994; compared to the giant we see today who has amassed significant amounts of wealth and esteem. Not to mention a massive gain for the overall stock prices.

The company went from a simple online bookstore to stocking electronics, gadgets, household items, and one of the biggest sellers of online books, audiobooks, and making huge deals with partners to promote their company. And interestingly enough, it even managed to secure contracts with government agencies like the CIA. This is no ordinary feat and could only be done with time, effort, and much patience.

Interestingly enough, the rise in stock price took significant jumps only in the last decade. It went public in 1997 and showed okay performance with a share price of $18, to begin with. You can see it's nothing to write home about. And they had insurmountable challenges as Jeff Bezos steered the company through the turbulent 1999/2000 dot com boom that threatened all online businesses. Many of which did not survive but Amazon did due to its unique selling proposition and loyal customer base. You may be surprised to find that Amazon did not make profit until 2001. That's almost seven years of being in business before seeing any form of benefit. And most companies would seek out opportunities for debt during this phase, but they decided to invest whatever revenue they had back into the business, finally seeing some traction in 2002.

Their star has been rising over time. And the trend indicates that there have been consistent rises in the stock over 20 years. If you considered the stock price in 2007, you could see that the stock price is $38.20, and that's almost two times the starting price in 1997 when first listed. From here on, you can see massive changes along the way, and right about 2015; Amazon's stock was gaining enormous traction and did not look to be stopping at all. They had reached a share price of $374.28 in 2015, and as you know, the price has hit $2317.80 by 2020.

What you must understand is that businesses take time to see these significant price updates, but they also evolve and learn with the times too. Amazon has been investing heavily in emerging technologies, including artificial intelligence and face recognition software. They also try new things all the time to improve customer service while also looking at creating world-class partnerships along the way.

Amazon is an excellent example of a company that started small and grew over time. And with this growth, there has been growth for its investors too. To round things off, let's look at a visual representation of the Amazon 10 years chart as found on capital.

I hope that this illustration shows you the potential of looking long term instead of a short time when it comes to stocks. And of course, there are countless examples I can share, but the final example I want to get across is about a company and CEO you know or may have heard a lot about.

This company is called Microsoft.

Microsoft stocks and their journey through time

This is a company that ranks only second to Amazon in cloud computing and has made its income through direct business integration worldwide. The stocks themselves are quite expensive and there, of course, is a reason for this. Microsoft has made a significant investment in the likes of cloud computing, LinkedIn, and Azure. All in all, they have been fine-tuning their business, investing in future real estate that will leave a legacy for the company. You can safely say that this company has grown from strength to strength as they invest in future technologies that yield game-changing results, but this was not always the case. It's good to note that the Microsoft journey was quite different from Amazon.

In 1980 to 2000 an incredible tech boom coupled. PC becoming the go-to mechanism to run business and the productive flagship programs like its office suite and operating system, this generated significant amounts of cash and revenue consistently. Keep in mind that many events took a turn for the worse during 2002, and they lost out to tech innovations like smartphones, media players, and tablets, which were headed by other companies in the tech space like Apple, Sony, and more. They did however look more intelligently at the market and as I mentioned in the start of this section they invested in applications like LinkedIn and Skype. They also started to embrace mobile technology allowing their office suite to become standard software on android devices. Overall their investors have been very happy with this shift and the price of the share has increased significantly over time. I'm sure you're curious about how the stock has shifted over time, let's consider this data now.

As mentioned in 2000, the share price was $45, and around about 2010, the share price for Microsoft was $28.18. This dip was likely due to the new technologies during this period. But this was also followed by an upward trajectory that led to the stock price at $180.76 at present.

The Microsoft example is an interesting one, where they started well and was the industry leader for years, only to have fallen behind the curve when new tech companies surfaced, and mobile became a norm. Yet they took a different approach and invested in future technologies like AI and cloud computing that saw them have massive gains. This has been the best time for investors when it comes to their Microsoft investment, and it looks set to rise even further in the future.

Key takeaways

- Different companies can follow a variety of pathways to become successful and increase their stock price. Sometimes time is the only factor that helps you make the right decision. Watching a stock week on week will not give you the key insights you need to make the right decision.
- Apple has been stable for years, but they had their ups and downs too, but with all the changes, it remains a leader in ensuring their shareholders achieve the best dividends and gains on their stocks.
- Similarly, Microsoft was always an industry leader but had a dip because of a tech boom they did not anticipate. Yes, they made up for it, and they continue to be market leaders that are more than generous with their payouts to their investors, and the investors are happier than ever. This could only have happened over the long term.
- Finally, Amazon is the reigning champion when it comes to success stories of success. The company only really started to see massive gains since 2015, and their star has been on the rise ever since. Keep in mind that if you had judged amazon 20 years ago, you might not have invested, so it's imperative to look at the future of a company and then make a decision.

Action steps

- Ensure you understand the trends of competent companies like Amazon and Apple so that you can apply this to other companies when researching.
- Consider looking at other company trends and discussing the patterns with a friend or relative.
- Most importantly, remember to use research in finding the best companies to invest in.

I want to leave you with my thoughts on this process of long term patterns in history. And the first is that patience is key and understanding that companies take time to grow. If you're willing to grow with these companies, they will help increase your shares immensely.

It's about time, we moved onto the next topic on our schedule, and that is an expansion of companies that have potential and will give you the best returns. In the next chapter, it will be vital that we look at low risk and companies with intrinsic values for your investments. You may recall that we considered intrinsic value companies in chapter 4, and now it's time to explore these companies in more detail.

VII
History

I've found over time that the best returns are likely to come via low risk and intrinsic companies that I know will not fail over 10 to 15 years. The one thing I am sure of is that you should make long term investments over the short term ones.

Warren Buffett famously said:

"Remember that the stock market is a manic depressive."

And his intention, of course, was to indicate to people that the market will go up and down, yet it should not worry you as long as you have invested with good companies, who you know offer a low risk and an excellent vehicle for your investment.

Even so, on many occasions, when I engage with people, they would rather invest their money in a 401K instead of waiting it out for 10 to 15 years for a strategy that is destined to work provided you use the right elements to drive it there. Indeed, you don't have much work to do when it comes to waiting it out except being patient, but the first move you have to make is ensuring you choose good companies in the first place. That's where most investors fail.

You may be thinking right now, but how do I know if the company is good or not?

This is the question you are getting an answer to in this chapter. I've shared some insight into this by looking at a variety of companies that performed well over a 10 and 20 year period. Herein lies the answer to knowing. It becomes more and more apparent that your investment increases over time when you invest in companies that will not fail. You must consider the characteristics of a good company and apply this to companies you look into for investing. Usually, the companies that have a high chance of succeeding will cross all the requirements you need.

So In this section, I'd like to take that a step further and go deeper into understanding what it means to find a good company. Also, I want to give you the clues and pathways to seeing these companies and what you should look for in your search.

Lesson topics

- What's low-risk intrinsic value means and how to leverage these companies
- Understand which companies are low risk and have intrinsic values and learn how to spot those golden companies that will mature later on
- How to understand the difference between a good company and a poor one

Contents

- The bull market and the story of a failed company

- Characteristics of a good company
- Intrinsic Value Companies
- My investments
- Takeaways
- Actions steps

Bull markets and the story of a failed company

Thinking about the last chapters, I've aimed to keep it very positive and steered clear from showing you failures in business. Arguably, learning about the failed companies is how you improve your knowledge of investing. In this chapter, you will find a single story about failed companies, but before you get there, you must understand a key term known as a 'Bull market.' If you've ever researched investing, you surely would have seen this phrase come up.

You should know that in the last decade, there has been something called a bull market.

What does that mean?

Definition Alert - A bull market is a term used in investment, and it indicates that an investment's price is rising over time. It can be related to stocks, bonds, and commodities too. The term is a metaphor of the thrust of a bull as it thrusts it's horns up in the air. And this is symbolic of what the market does. When a bull market starts, it's a good symbol showing economic expansion is about to hit.

And generally, over the last ten years, many companies have performed above average, yet some companies have not. The reality of business is that only 25% of companies in the US survive 15 years or more.

Many companies look great on paper, only to perform dismally over an extensive period. These companies can be found far and wide. I have not put a broad focus on these companies, as I wanted to show you success stories. Yet I'm going to share a story of a company you may have heard of that seemed like a good company. But it failed to realize the gains necessary for its shareholders.

You may remember that I discussed the entertainment company Netflix in an earlier chapter, and of course, the innovation that came from Netflix resulted in a big company called Blockbuster being unable to keep up. Before Netflix came around, rented movies were viewed via video cassette or on DVD, and Blockbuster was the leader in Canada and the US. Starting in 1985, they enjoyed market leader status over the next two decades. If you look at their standing in 2010, you will see that the company had to file bankruptcy because nobody was watching DVDs or video cassettes any longer. Netflix had simply made it easier to watch movies in the comfort of your home.

Mainly the founder of Netflix Reed Hasting was frustrated by the late fees that Blockbuster was charging. Blockbuster made 16% of its income from late payments, so he decided to start Netflix and charge no late fees at all. Their first mistake came in 2000 when they had the opportunity to buy Netflix for $50 million, but they declined. Ironically Netflix became their most significant competitor and the main reason they went out of business. As you can imagine, this company had seen great share prices over time, yet due to not following the trends and heeding their market, they failed to innovate as had other companies like Apple and

Microsoft. Sadly, the shareholders of that company made a loss too. This can be avoided for you as a new investor by looking to those companies that meet the characteristics of a good company.

Characteristics of a good company

It's good to know that there are companies that you should not invest in because it will save you from losing money and becoming frustrated with your investment journey. And similarly, like there are failing companies, there are hugely successful ones too. And at this point, more innovative companies keep coming onto the scene, aiming to add value and turn a profit for the shareholders.

Ultimately you always want to be thinking about having a reliable company to handle your investment. Think of it this way; you're handing over money to a company that you earned or worked relatively hard for. Therefore you only want professionals to be dealing with your funds. In this way, you need to consider companies that have a vested interest in creating value for the shareholders and ensuring they always provide the best returns on investment.

I've listed the main characteristics of a good company to invest in:

The company has limited competition

You must look at the leading players in the industry that your potential investment lies in. Some industries are heavily saturated, and this could be an alarm bell for you.

When a company has few competitors, this would often be due to high barriers of entry, or the company has differentiated itself so much that it's hard for others to do what they do. In doing so, they have a sort of monopoly on the market for the foreseeable future. I want you to consider these companies as a starting point that has very little competition due to this crucial differentiation characteristic.

One current example that has investors excited is **Novocure.** This is an alternative treatment for cancer that works in conjunction with current cancer protocols. At present, they are the only makers of this noninvasive device that has been patented and approved by the FDA. This works with a variety of other illnesses too. Their flagship product is Octune.

Let's now consider another characteristic to look out for when considering investing in a company.

The company has an easily recognizable brand

Companies like Apple, Samsung, and Tesla have done a brilliant job of marketing their brand extensively. It's become easily recognizable, and consequently, you trust the brand more. Always be looking out for brands with a strong presence in all mediums. These brands are investing heavily in attention, and this is taking their brand to audiences all over the world. An excellent place to start is to search Google, look at the news stories about them, and follow them on their social media channels. You may also want to look at their product reviews to get a sense of the market they operate in and their customer sentiment.

Considering Apple, Steve Jobs has always been evident and precise in his presentation of the product, pioneering apple launches, building excitement, getting the apple brand out there. The rule of thumb is that if it's easily recognizable, it's worth looking into as a potential investment. And that has changed slightly since Tim Cook took over. Yet there is the ongoing brand of authority that will maintain for years to come. Their name is synonymous with a sense of passion, creativity, and powerful interplays of technology that are future focused. This consistently attracts people who want to associate with such characteristics to the brand. You would also consider apple a high authority brand, which is in a medium to expensive market catering to more affluent users. They have gone out of their way to get celebrities to become early adopters of their gadgets, and this is another aspect of the power of their brand and how quickly it is recognized globally.

And you may also want to consider the next characteristic of a good company, and that is how much return on the capital they are currently experiencing.

Return on capital

This indicator shows how successful a company is at turning invested capital into profits. It's a useful tool that can help you measure the potential growth in a company. A higher return on equity compared to a competitor means a company is doing something right to grow their profits and may be worth taking a second look. Return on capital becomes more important for companies who invest large amounts of money as you saw with

Microsoft, who spent billions into the AI industry. These investments take time to mature, but if you consider Microsoft's current return on capital, it's sitting in the high 80 percent as of writing. This is a great place to be for a company. Other firms like oil and gas companies also invest a large amount of capital. And it should be your duty to know how your company uses your money, as it will be a key indicator if you will get an excellent or poor return on your investment.

The company has loyal customers

Since loyal customers are likely to be repeat customers, it's essential to understand the customer base of a company you wish to invest in. Also, consider that the cost to acquire new customers is considerably more expensive than marketing to current customers.

To give you more insight, a study was done by Morning Consult on the companies with the most loyal customer base. Interestingly enough, the top 2 of the list have an excellent reputation and are opportunities to invest. The first is Wal-Mart, and the second is Amazon.

A strong management team

This aspect may take time to understand or figure out, but consider that a successful company needs proper management to keep it going. If they do have an excellent track record, then you can see the management team working well for the company.

Yet, if you do notice a shift in management, it would be a good idea to investigate and understand the new management that is on board and their relevant track records. Change management is often involved when the new administration takes over and could upset the current success of the company. The new managers should be leaders in their field and have excellent track records running this company too.

While there isn't a unique formula to assess strong management, but there are factors that you should look into. One such factor is to check the strategy and goals of the company and check for conciseness.

A good company will have a jargon-free mission statement, and also have set goals that keep the management moving forward. Another aspect to consider is the compensation for high-level executives and look at it compared to others in the same industry.

Look at the company's balance sheet

Since publicly traded companies provide the company's balance, you can always get a sense of the company's outlook. While most investors focus on the income statement, make sure you look at the company's balance sheet for a good indication of future success.

The balance will make you aware of shortfalls that could potentially impact the success of the company over the next ten years.

You now have an excellent idea of a successful company and its characteristics to look out for investing, let's consider a critical aspect in terms of a company's performance.

You always want to invest in a company with the best performance, and this is how you know that a company is performing well.

- **The revenue is growing over time** - This is simply done by looking at the company's overall profit and loss statement. An increase in income over time is a good sign. A good indicator is to look year on year, and this can also be found online with a trended view for you. Stay away from declines over some time. Look at overall profitability, and it will keep you moving in the right thought pattern, knowing that this company looks excellent financially now and in the future.

- **The expenses are staying flat** - Of course, with a growth in a company, costs will rise. Yet it should increase relative to the company's revenue. In other words, the curve of expenses stays flat.

- **Your Debt Ratios Should Be Low** - Look for the solvency ratios of a company. This will show your debt versus your company's value. It's best to find a low cost, which is 2:1 being ideal.

These are key indicators that a company is doing well and always look at that before, making that unique decision to move ahead.

So what I'm hoping to bring across is that you should steer clear from average companies that do not have any of these characteristics and show excellent performance. The better you know a company and the literature there is about a company. The better it is to do the necessary research and get an excellent understanding of this company as a whole. Most of this data is available through the brokerage you use as well as the internet if they are publicly traded companies.

Now, I want you to focus ahead and move into the field of intrinsic value companies.

Intrinsic Value Companies

You've got a good solid background of low-risk companies and their characters, and what to look out for, now it's time to look at intrinsic value companies such as companies that will never go out of style in your lifetime.

What are the so-called intrinsic value companies?

You may remember that we looked at this briefly in chapter 4, and now I want us to take a more extensive look so that we can bed down these companies and discover how you can find them.

An intrinsic value company is one that has substantial value, and you will see returns on these companies in the long term. This is useful for investors as it gives you a sense of what to expect. There are many different ways to calculate the intrinsic value of a company.

The economist does give us an indication that the current value of how much cash flow available is the intrinsic value. Yet others think specific criteria should be met for it to be an intrinsic value company.

You can start by looking at the discounted cash flow analysis. This is indicated using the time value of money. Also, consider what the company seems to see coming in terms of cash flow.

Another good one is to look at a variety of metrics. You can check out the price to earnings ratio to give you a good idea.

And finally, you may consider the asset-based valuation. This is often used where you simply take all the assets and subtract liabilities.

Intrinsic value companies are beneficial because they give you as an investor a sense of surety in your investment. You feel less at risk, know the company is suitable and will remain that way for the near future. Remember that your goal is always to get the intrinsic value so you can look for stocks selling less than what they are worth in terms of future growth. Eventually, this lower price stock you bought finally matures, and you reach your aim. And it all starts by finding that inherent value to the company.

My investments

While Warren Buffet may have dumped his Airline stock, I've invested heavily in airline stock. The big four US airline stocks include Delta, American, United, and Southwest. And it's important to know that they have around about 80% of the market share. One major arrear of concern, of course, has been the COVID-19 pandemic, which has tanked most stocks. Yet, it looks to be a resurgence soon once we have gotten control of the problem at hand.

Another thing I did notice is that sometimes airlines do expand the coverage, and there's always this fear from fellow investors that it would drop the share prices due to rivals and competition and so forth. That said, always look out for unit revenue on airline stocks, as it helps to determine both efficiency and profitability. That simply means that if the price of the seat is much lower than the standard rate due to discounts applied, even if the occupancy is high - the unit revenue average will give a low indicator. And while COVID-19 is with us, these numbers would be severely affected, but they soon will improve, and the stocks will undoubtedly rise again.

I also have a stake in cruise lines and Boeing investments from an Airplane company. You may be curious to know how this works, so let me break everything down for you.

Let's start with cruise lines. I've found that there are many benefits of owning cruise line stocks, and I'm going to highlight for you below.

But firstly, let me explain what they might be.

There are four main cruise lines, namely Carnival Corp, Carnival plc, and Royal Caribbean Cruises limited, and Norwegian Cruise line holdings limited. For the sake of convenience, let's make the carnival group as one.

These stocks can be bought, and basically, the shareholder gets free onboard credit when using the cruise lines. That's a bonus. Yet these stocks have been known to have had some turbulent times (like now). But they have genuinely risen in value, and I've seen my shares see some healthy growth along the way.

Lastly, I also want to share my investments in an Airplane company called Boeing, perhaps you've heard about it.

The Boeing Company makes and sells airplanes, rockets, and missiles globally. It's one of the largest aerospace manufacturers. They also committed to using more electric powered sources for their aero technology over time.

This is, of course, a way to remain sustainable. Over time my stock has increased gradually to $319. There haven't been miserable months when owning a Boeing share, and they take care of their shareholders. This is an example of an intrinsic, low-risk stock that you can put your money behind.

Key takeaways

- The reality is that there is very low risk when you invest in a company over the long term. Remember, as the company grows, so too does your shares.
- You want to consider a suitable intrinsic value, such as the examples highlighted for you, such as the Boeing company. Airline companies and cruise lines. And while they may not be looking great right now - they will be sure to rise again.
- And finally, choose reputable companies instead of unknown ones, keep searching until you find a company that has the marking of a good business and it will bring you gains on your investment.

Action steps

- Research and note down five low-risk companies you would invest in provided you had the means.
- Find out everything there is to know about these five companies, including matching them up with the characteristics you learned about in this section.
- Check that you have signed up for the online brokerages I shared in chapter 4, like Robinhood or TD Ameritrade.

Overall this chapter was sharing important, vital information you must know about trustworthy and competent companies to invest in. I wanted to share success stories, but I also wanted to show you a company like Blockbuster that seemed to be winning, but they did not keep up with the times and went bankrupt. And all of the shareholders were left in the lurch. This is not a scenario I recommend or want for you. Therefore, I also shared substantial shares that you must consider that I have invested in and saw massive gains.

And now that you have critical insights into low risk and intrinsic value companies and how to leverage them, let's move forward to the action of finally investing. I'm confident that this chapter and the ones before have given you the confidence and inspiration to start your investment journey, and that's exactly what we'll do next.

VIII

Game Time

You made it to the action stage, and indeed it has been an exciting road filled with discoveries and compelling insights along the way. In writing this book, I've always aimed to give you the details you need to feel empowered on your journey through investing. I want to share a story with you that made me into leap investing. Before being a serial investor, I always prided myself on being the star employee who would go the extra mile.

I was the highest achiever, and every year I aimed to push forward and do better. The promotions came quickly. I found every advancement would cause my workload to increase, and my time was slowly disappearing. I had insufficient time to do the things I loved to do, and indeed I was making enough money to live a beautiful life, but I was short on passion, excitement, and a nest egg to finally retire young and be financially free.

I made this realization little by little, and instead of taking dramatic steps like walking into my manager's office, I decided to be smart in my approach. I knew that I needed to be employed to earn an income, and I also knew that I could treat my job as just a job, not a 15-hour workday. Interestingly enough, when I started working my regular work hours, great things began to happen. For one, I became 10 times more productive, and also I had time to search out opportunities to invest in, and my knowledge of investing grew over time.

Eventually, I sat at this point where you might be right now. You've learned everything you need to get started, you have all the resources, and now it's up to you to take action.

Action is undoubtedly essential when investing, but more important is consistent action. It's said that anyone can take action when they feel great, and the world is fantastic, but real investing champions do it when it's tough and challenging too. This is what helps you to see the results you have been longing for finally.

So how do you finally start investing?

The good news is that in this chapter, you will get into action mode, and you will start your first investment. This is a chapter all about action and will show how committed you are to building a nice nest egg for yourself in 10-15 years as your stocks mature. Let's take it step-by-step, and if you follow along, I'm entirely confident you will have invested your first sum of money by the end of this chapter.

Lesson topics

- How to invest in your brokerage account and still make winnings at the end
- You will have the ability to purchase a stock and own one if you follow the indicated for you.

- You will have diversified your portfolio of stocks available to you and from the comfort of your phone or laptop.
- You surely don't have to waste your time and money on a 401K, nor will you be bothered by the fluctuations and or stress associated.

Contents

- Deposit a lump sum of cash into a brokerage account
- Make small deposits every week.
- Diversify your portfolio
- Forget the 401K.

Deposit a lump sum of cash into a brokerage account

This first step may be challenging for some because it's not easy always to have a lump sum of cash available to invest at the drop of a hat.

From my perspective, I've personally made a lot of strategic investments, and what helped me was that I knew that I needed to deposit into my account every week. This was a habit I knew instinctively I needed to form, and it was a beneficial one. You perhaps know how 'emergencies' crop up for money all the time.

It all started with that initial sum of money, and I haven't looked back since. Initially, it was a challenge finding this lump sum as I had responsibilities and was entirely new to the field. Yet, I knew there was a shift of mindset needed to make it a reality indeed. I could see that I was willing to part with my money for the latest fashion trends, but I could not invest. This showed me where my priorities were at that moment. I had to take drastic measures auditing my expenses, and amazingly enough; I found areas I could use to fund my first sum of cash for investing.

Make small deposits every week

I like to deposit a percentage every week for the best results, so in a sense, you could say that my investment portfolio has become my savings account. As opposed to a regular savings account, I can expect that my investment portfolio will keep on multiplying over time. You could look at your brokerage account in the same way, and most good ones don't charge commissions like they used to, so that's the first bonus for you.

In the first step or as the beginning, I want you to focus your mind on using your brokerage account with Robinhood to TD Ameritrade, as mentioned previously. These are the most convenient for someone who is just starting.

Once you've signed up with your preferred brokerage, you're all set to go and ready to deposit a lump sum of cash into your brokerage account. Say, for example, you have earned an income of $1000 and saved to begin your first investment adventure. You wouldn't merely dive into investing. It's essential to look at some of the stocks that will bring you the most return. We talked a lot about how to recognize those stocks looking only at companies with intrinsic value and that are low risk.

You want to ensure a reputable company is getting your hard-earned cash and working for you. From here, you want to consider having a small amount deposited into your brokerage account every week, perhaps committing to a percentage that will build a nice some that can be used for your investments when the time is just right. Think about it now, it's been a time when many high stocks have fallen, so if you want to build up your portfolio, you're setting yourself up to get in on the buy low and sell high strategy which will take flight for you.

If you're a student, how do you fund this account?

Consider your allowance or your money from your side hustle. There are so many exciting ways to make money right now as a young adult.

I'm going to list a few ideas for you:

- In the early stages, you could work extra hours at your job for overtime when they are offering. Many companies require additional staff for evening shifts, and this could be a great opportunity.
- If you are quite creative, you could take stock photography and sell these to stock websites. You can check out Shutterstock or Dreamstime.
- Manage social media for small businesses

I have not included driving for Lyft or Uber, and this may be an option for you in the future for you. These are simple yet effective ways to create an extra $100 or more a month to fund that investment account.

Do you have an extra $100 every week that can be funneled away into your brokerage account, and coupled with the current $1000, you keep growing this amount. I've mentored a few graduates in the art of investing and building up the capital first to make that substantial investment when it becomes available. Many have worked as freelancers while they study. So they would be at college during the day and after 8 pm their second job would start.

For example, they would make an income of $200 that week, perhaps using Photoshop to create logos for a customer of a client. This money or portion can then be channeled every week into their brokerage account. As an added tip, make it automatic and set a percentage every Friday of the week for money to quickly go into that account.

Once you've funded the brokerage account with an amount of your choosing, it's time to start getting into the stocks you will be buying at a low price, and keeping for an extended period. You may have $500, $1000, or more so you'll be ready to keep your ear to the ground as more and more companies share updates, put on alerts of stocks from your phone, and check it every single day. Read the news and follow investing accounts on twitter, which share updates on how the markets and good companies are looking from all aspects. And of course, if you keep up to date with current affairs, you will have a good idea as to how the economy is doing and what the big names like Apple, Coca-Cola, Microsoft, and Amazon are getting up to.

And once you start to see some changes in the market, it means your real investing work begins. As such, now the market is exploding with opportunity. The economy is set to hit a recession due to COVID-19. There are so many companies where the stocks have hit an all-time low. You will never get that price again, and when you do your due diligence and purchase that stock, you can simply add it to your portfolio. Of course, you should not put all your eggs in one basket; you must diversify that portfolio and keep on adding stocks as you find them. This process is never-ending but also exciting as you research, listen, and look out for new shares that can add value to your portfolio.

Of course, you should be extremely disciplined, ensuring your funds from your brokerage account are only used for the best stock that is sure to bring you returns in the future. You must ensure that you do not get sucked into the emotional high of the market place or following the crowd. This can happen, and it's been proven time and time again. A form of groupthink starts to take place, and people follow leaders with the answers blindly during a crisis.

This should not be your approach. Always think carefully, and remember that patience is critical in your strategy. Since you will be waiting for your stock to mature for at least 10-15 years, what's a few hours or days spent looking into all the critical company info of a stock. It can save you so much grief in the long run when you decide to purchase shares that are hands-down winners, and you get them at the best rate.

Diversify your portfolio

So what's the key to diversifying your portfolio?

I have seen so many new investors open a brokerage account, add money into it, and then suddenly, they have accumulated 10-15 different stocks without much thought. Eventually, they sit with the stock but do not know if it will perform at the level needed, more so it's not reputable companies either.

Let's now look at diversifying that portfolio of yours. Let's say you have $1000 to invest, and you've added this to your brokerage account at either Robin hood or TD Ameritrade. Yet your aim is not to but it all into one basket. You want to spread it out well. Perhaps you noticed in the previous section that Microsoft stock is looking good and has been on an upward trend over time. You also consider their future investments, and it seems like they would be a great bet. You decide to invest $300 in Microsoft and then $100 into Apple as well. But you think that maybe the performance will also be a problem over time even though you're confident in the companies, but just as a backup, you go ahead and invest in 1 more stock for Facebook.

This diversification allows you to spread the risk, and now you have the three stocks available to watch and wait it out for the long term. Over time, and as you gain more finances from your job or business, you will find that you treat your brokerage account as a savings account like I do, and the only difference for me is that it brings me a return.

And while you've got a solid understanding of investing in stocks and getting started, I'd like to caution you against a common misunderstanding right now.

Forget the 401K

In my experience, which I shared earlier in this chapter, a 401K is a waste of time and money that could have been invested in the stock market.

The misconception is that your 401K will be your retirement vehicle and that you show continue heaping money into it. It's simply not the case. Perhaps it may have been so many decades ago. Things have changed dramatically, and now that you understand the details of the investment puzzle, you'll notice the following.

The wealthy never use a 401K to get rich or build their wealth because they know that it is severely limited and will be taxed using the income tax rates. Also, consider that your 401K can not be used until you reach 59.5 of age. And imagine how limited the interest is on it, severely limited that all you end up doing is paying for the management fees of your 401K and handling fees. And while it may be easy to use and connected to your employer, it means less work from your side. But the income you lose along the way is significant too.

I urge you to steer clear of 401K's in favor of the investing model I have shared with you, and that is start by using stocks to build your investments and diversify your portfolio. Be ready to be in it for the long haul, but know that you can always cash out when you choose instead of wait 20/30/40 years to use the funds. In a sense, you will have full control of your money.

Yes, so you have come so far, and at this stage, you may be feeling a sense of trepidation. And perhaps you fired up your brokerage account and transferred funds to start investing. You're wondering if this will be worth it and if you'll have the patience to wait it out.

Perhaps you also think that if you do not do it, then when will you finally start investing.

I can tell you that starting now using what you have is the key to success with investing. You will always look back at this moment and feel like you should have made it happen. And you will see stocks years later for prominent legacy-driven companies like Apple and wish you had made the first step by starting with Robinhood and Ameritrade.

I can say, of course, that it's not too late, and you can do it right now.

Key takeaways

- Please know that your money does nothing in a 401K or savings account, and it only makes your company or your bank more money which they lend out to loan seekers for an interest rate. You could instead leverage your money and make it work for you through smart investments that take no less than 30-45 minutes of your day to get started. It's the best action you will ever take, and perhaps people may find your new habit weird; that's ok as you will be smiling in 10 years as your investments start to form into your retirement plan.
- Keep in mind that you can invest as much money as you can in a company and hold it for years. As I've shown you throughout this book, companies are living and breathing, but over time they start to make a considerable consistent increase. During those years, that company will keep doing well, and the stock price will gradually increase over time.

- So yes, I'm saying you can make money while you sleep, and finally achieve that goal of early retirement.

Next steps

- You have to get something into the investing game, start small even $100 can make a difference. This will be a starting point for you.
- Start checking into your online brokerage daily for 10-15 minutes until it becomes a habit. Think of it like browsing your social media
- Read an investment book, start small, and aim to read about 15-20 pages every day.

You know the best feeling I've experienced recently is that I make money while I sleep. I wake up every day and see how amazing my portfolio looks, and I think back to how my investment has grown. I know I have a significant nest egg available to me when I finally retire. It's such a profound change from working in a 9-5 job, hoping that all of your hard work comes to something. Now I can confidently say that I control my future and my financial freedom. If this is something you will feel, then the process is highlighted within these pages for you, and it's all about taking one step forward towards investing.

Perhaps it means stop overthinking and start doing. Maybe it means finding something to remove from your life that is costing enormous sums of money and using that for your first investment. I suppose what I'm hoping to get across is that you simply have to start.

That said, I think it's about time we finally head over to chapter 9, where I'll be discussing in detail how you can make money while you sleep.

IX
Residual Income

Imagine waking up and finding that you have a massive sum of money in your bank account. You knew that you did not work for it, but somehow you had this money. You think about the fact that your company may have sent you the wrong salary, or you won the lottery.

Yet, for many people everywhere, they wake up to deposits into their accounts every day. And it's for sure they don't think it was by luck. It's all by intent, and they know exactly where the money came from. They have successfully done the thing people dream about, the idea that offers you almost 2 million search results on Google. Yes, I'm talking about how to make money in your sleep.

Spoiler alert, you can experience this feeling too. And it's often known as passive income, and the reason we can finally talk about this is that you have come full circle on your investing journey.

It's time to reap the rewards and make the dreams of retiring young and doing it while you are still healthy to enjoy everything this life has to offer. This chapter will open your eyes to how one percent of the population of the world currently lives and hopefully inspire you to join us, becoming financially free.

Lesson topics

- Detailed ideas and concepts about passive income and how you can make it
- Why making money in your sleep is necessary for early retirement and living your dream life.
- How to finally get out of that paycheck to paycheck cycle and have financial freedom
- Holding long term stocks will keep you confident in your financial future.
- Patience is vital when on your journey to passive income.

Contents

- Passive income is the key to wealth
- Making money while you sleep is so important
- If you trade time for money (9-5 job), you will always be living paycheck to paycheck and will never have financial freedom
- You need to know how to set yourself up for success
- When you hold long term, you don't even need to check the balance
- Just be patient and know that in 10 or so years, when you want to make changes in your life, that the money you invested will be multiplied and that multiplication factor will determine your wealth.

Yet have you ever wondered what precisely passive income might be?

Gary Vaynerchuck, an entrepreneur on Instagram and YouTube, says that there is no such thing as passive income.

Also keep in mind that on the other end of the spectrum of this topic, we have one of the leading players of passive income that tells us that:

"If you don't find a way to make money while you sleep, you will work until you die."

You may have heard his name before. Yes, he is the renowned investor, Warren Buffet.

Yet, I think it will pay to take a deep dive into passive income and what it could mean for you and your goals to retire young, vibrant, and wealthy. In short passive income is money you earn without needing to work for that money every single day as you do with a job. It could mean you invest cash up front and work, but you can leave the money to do the work.

This is what the strategy I teach in this book is about; it's about getting to levels of passive income that allow you to wake up daily and find notifications that your portfolio has increased over time, your wealth is growing year on year. Overall you can tell that passive income is the key to real wealth that the likes of Warren Buffet, Grant Cardone, and others have.

These individuals are wealthy because of their substantial investment early on in life, and now as they are older, they don't have to worry about money in any way or form. They are sorted for growth and earning passive income.

Many people have different ways of creating passive income for themselves, and all are valid. Yet, for your purposes, I want to teach you how to do it using a simple process of investing in the stock market using the technologies at your disposal. I want to take your mind to the previous chapter, where you learned how to invest in a brokerage account slowly. And from here, build your capital, and once done, you always have the security and means to buy a stock that meets the criteria for an intrinsic value but low-risk company.

This fund and purchasing your low-risk stock is only the beginning. Let's face it; you've invested your $1000 or however much you may have spent, and now comes the waiting. It could be ten years or 15 years. Are you ready for this and will you be mature and patient enough to push through. My sense is that now that you understand the details of the stock market and the simplicity of the methodology of buying low and selling high - you will be more than patient to multiply that initial investment for your future. I've recently purchased stocks in 2020 and truly capitalized on the current pandemic and the lack of people investing. And I intend to keep this stock right up to 2035. It would be foolish of me to sell this stock without it achieving full maturity.

Overall, the future has few options right now. You attend university or college and graduate, and from here, you enter the workplace where you will likely be starting at an entry-level position. Generally, that's the starting point if you can find a job that is. At the current climate, unemployment rates have skyrocketed, and people are struggling to meet their basic needs. So let's say you are in the rat race, and then you will be asked to invest in a retirement fund like a 401K. And while there, you will work long hours to get ahead and make that promotion. But that certainly cannot be your life for the next 40-50 years.

As you discovered in the previous chapter, your retirement fund is too little to survive on when you retire. Besides, you don't only want to survive; you want to live a life filled with meaning and experiences when you are young enough and healthy enough to appreciate it sincerely. You cannot get rich while working a regular job; the system was not designed that way. You always need to work to get a set output of money and to increase your income you must work more. Since you only have 24 hours in a day, then your income is capped. You'll have to broaden your mind and find another means to create wealth for yourself. The way is through investing in the stock market for extended times so that while you do have to work, you also have a backup plan that is creating enormous wealth for you so you and your loved ones can retire at 35 to 40. At present, the retirement age is 65, and after 65 years of age, even then, our parents don't have enough to enjoy their final days. And the only way to shift this cycle is to think differently and change the game for you. Your foray into investment will be the tool that will help you to ditch your job and finally achieve financial freedom that lets you make all the right decisions on how you want to spend your life. You will embrace the idea that Warren Buffet shared that you have to find out how to make money while you sleep. And this is the answer.

And please do not misunderstand me, I'm certainly not saying that you should quit your job or say no to job offers because the system is not working. I am saying that you should plan for your success.

While you work, make sure you also save for your future in a nontraditional way. Do it through investing in stocks that will guarantee you a return on your investment. Invest in your education about the stocks and invest your money for a future you may not be able to see right now but one you hope for.

In totality, it's now a decision you need to take on the way forward. You have the available tools and resources at your disposal. There is also a good understanding of the best methods to invest your money.

And keep in mind that you know the detailed plan on how to do it. All that's left is to get the income to create your first purchase of stock. I can tell you this, though, that once you start on this investment journey; you will not even need to check your balance anymore. You will be confident and secure in your plan and waiting patiently for everything to materialize.

Finally, as you review the characteristics and rewards of a truly passive income - know that you may need to be extra patient along the way. It does take up to 10/20 years to see the gains. At that time, you can keep building your funds to keep investing and growing your portfolio and creating an even bigger nest egg. The truth is you become wiser and more experienced in the art of investing. You'll start to learn the nuances and volatility associated with individual stocks, and you may even branch out to new brokerages or also get yourself a private broker due to a significant increase in your portfolio. The options are endless for the way forward for you. It's all about you and how well you play your cards in the initial stages.

Will you be willing to sacrifice now so you can reap the rewards later?

I know that I always wish I had started sooner, and I knew that if I did, I would have been a lot further on in my investment journey too. Don't get me wrong; I have certainly mastered the skills needed in picking the right stock for future growth, and I've helped others do the same, but I wish that I had this book when I started my journey.

What would I tell my younger self? Do it now. Later is too late, and you're leaving money on the table by not investing.

Key takeaways

- You've learned so much, but you should also consider that passive income is within your reach if you take the initiative to do the research, learning, and work upfront and be patient.
- Patience will be difficult, but as a student of discipline and smart strategic investments, you will get better at it as you start to see a growing portfolio.
- You will be inspired by the increased knowledge you have on investing that helps you find stocks quickly and get them into your portfolio.
- And finally INVEST NOW, sit back and enjoy the ride.

Action steps

- Invest now, and get started towards a more prosperous and fulfilling life

- Build your investment portfolio, diversify your income and keep growing until you are ready to cash out
- Keep reading, improving your knowledge and finding good companies to invest in

As the final chapter in this book, know that you are truly capable of making money while you sleep. Know that passive income is something that you can accumulate and know that you will never have to worry incessantly about being able to afford your retirement.

You will retire, young and vibrant, and you will probably thank your younger self for making those decisions and being patient along the way. Investing might be the only pure form of passive income still available to you.

Investing itself does not require the avid management of your stock portfolio once you've done the work of finding a suitable stock.

You simply earn money because you decided to invest in the best stock. Yet your only requirement is that you're patient. When you invest in the right stock, you will undoubtedly make back your investment and more in 10 years.

The only change to investing has been that more people are discovering a new way to create an income for themselves. Yet, I think what sets apart the successful investor from the unsuccessful one is delayed gratification and putting in the work to find a lucrative stock in the first place.

My philosophy remains that you buy low, sell high, and ensure you only invest in reputable companies and have the patience to wait it out long term.

X
Farewell

Thank you so much for coming along on this exciting journey that introduced you to investing while you're still young. This is the ultimate beginner guide to investment that I wish I had when I was younger.

I've read so many books on investing, and I can tell you that when you're done, you are just as confused as to when you started. Let's face it, the world of investing used to be that it was for people who learned trade secrets and leveraged those secrets to make money.

Over time, there has been a considerable shift, and if you're willing and curious to expand your mind and think differently, you can leverage the power of investing your money for better gains in 10 and 15 years.

I always want to ensure that you gain the most from this book. When I set out writing the book, it was clear to me that many young people were hungry to start investing and was curious about it too.

Yet, it became all too clear that the current literature was not sufficient for new starters to investing. As an avid learner and teacher of investment strategies, I'm so happy to have shared this journey with you, where you now have the exact tools, resources, and thinking I used in my approach to investing.

You also have a clear plan on how to get started. You also know the standard platforms to make use of as well as the steps to take to start that investment cycle going. At the same time, you know that you should be in it for the long haul. There is a certain mindset associated with investing and being successful in it, and as the great investors of the world have always maintained:

Investing is a long game, and if you choose this path, you should be a very patient person. I read an excellent metaphor for investing, which I'd love to share with you right now.

Charles Ellis said: "Investing is a continuous process. It isn't supposed to be interesting; it's a responsibility. If you go to the stock market because you want excitement, sooner or later, you will lose."

As a student of investment, you must keep on learning every step of the way by mastering your mindset, preparing your income, and always researching and taking advantage of the current economic trends at present. Your aim should be to look at the current status of the world and yet also think about how you can still maximize your investment status. And I know once you shift your mindset to this approach, everything will click for you, and you will be equipped to take that first step, connecting your first round of funds to a brokerage and also buying your first stock.

I will always caution you to be patient, look at the information I shared, especially the detailed trends on the stock market fluctuations, learn how to read income statements, and practice understanding these. Your financial knowledge is like a key to unlock the best information on stocks to purchase for the future. Also remember that you should create a solid plan for yourself where you look at your life in 15 years, and imagine in vivid detail what that might be. Take note of this by writing it down; if it's your dream house, car, or travel destination, no matter the extravagance, write it down. You will find that this approach will set you motivation stirring to get the ball rolling for your investment strategy. You must plan for success in investing. Therefore, if you buy a stock in year 1, then you can expect to make a sale of that stock in year 15.

As for our journey, it must end here, but for you, you will always have this handy guide to help you on your investment journey.

Now that you've finished the book, it's truly time to get to work. Start by investing in your first stock, and then keep on sending funds to the brokerage account so you will always have the means to buy shares when times like the current pandemic happen again.

Action steps

- If you have not done so already, you must invest in your first stock and hold onto it for the long term.
- Keep your brokerage account funded so you will have sufficient funding to invest in future opportunities.
- Start now, later is too late.

The first thing that you have to be proud of is that you have taken your financial future into your own hands, You've made it right through to the end of this book which shows that you certainly want to achieve a financially free life that lets you live by your own rules. Investing is a long term solution to your challenges that is the potential to let you do many things. These include things such as traveling, living healthier and happier, and spending time with those closest to you.

It's truly all in your hands, go forth and make that first investment so you can retire young and wealthy.

www.ingramcontent.com/pod-product-compliance
Lightning Source LLC
Chambersburg PA
CBHW060418220526
45465CB00008B/2929